PERFECT PITCH

PERFECT PITCH

100 PIECES of CLASSICAL MUSIC to Bring JOY, TEARS, SOLACE, EMPATHY, INSPIRATION (& EVERYTHING IN BETWEEN)

TIM BOUVERIE

Published in the UK in 2021 by Short Books
an imprint of Octopus Publishing Group Ltd
Carmelite House, 50 Victoria Embankment
London, EC4Y 0DZ

www.octopusbooks.co.uk
www.shortbooks.co.uk

An Hachette UK Company
www.hachette.co.uk

10 9 8 7 6 5 4 3 2 1

Copyright © Tim Bouverie 2021
Illustrations © Evie Dunne

A CIP catalogue record for this book is available from the British Library.

ISBN 978-1-78072-528-4

Printed and bound in Great Britain by Clays Ltd, Elcograf S.p.A

This FSC® label means that materials used for the
product have been responsibly sourced

Jacket design © Gray318

To Lydia, Genevieve and Clarissa,
with love and gratitude

'Music is a higher revelation than all
wisdom and philosophy.'
Ludwig van Beethoven

'Without music, life would be a mistake.'
Friedrich Nietzsche

Preface

This book emerged, by accident, during lockdown. Unable to access archives for the book I was (and am) meant to be writing on Allied diplomacy during the Second World War and wanting to spread a little joy in an increasingly depressing world, I decided to send a small group of friends a daily link to a favourite piece of classical music, along with a few lines of context and personal insight. Perhaps inevitably, the 'essays' grew in size and scope. More surprisingly, so did the distribution list, as friends asked me to include brothers, sisters, parents, lovers, friends of friends and colleagues. I seemed to have struck a chord: to have unearthed a longing not simply for classical music but a way into classical music. Slowly, the idea of writing a short book, shorn of technical terms, that would serve as an introduction to one hundred classical masterpieces took shape.

I am not a musician or a musicologist. Nor am I a historian of music. My field, so much as I have one, is politics and international relations between and during the two world wars. I have, however, nurtured a love of classical music since I was five years old; a childhood obsession with the works of George Frederick Handel, that led to an adoration of Bach, Beethoven and, above all, Mozart. Soon Schubert, Chopin, Schumann and Tchaikovsky were in the mix and, by the time I was at university, I was listening to Verdi and Wagner on alternate weeks. Not all music moved me. Although my taste steadily expanded from the early 18th century to the mid-

20th century, some composers left me cold. Readers may be shocked by omissions from my selection but I think there is something in the theory that to really love certain works of art means, almost by definition, to have a distaste for others – to appreciate all is to appreciate none. This, therefore, is not a list of the 'greatest' or 'most important' pieces of classical music (even if such a list were possible). Nor is it an inventory of my 'Top 100' pieces. It is simply a compilation of music which I love and think that others will love too. Classical music, it is my passionate belief, has the capacity to move and be enjoyed by almost anyone, yet too often people are overwhelmed by the sheer size and alleged complexity of the canon. Where to start? What to listen to? And what does it all mean? Idiosyncratic and impressionistic, this is a brief attempt to answer these questions.

Tim Bouverie, June 2021

Contents

1

Dido and Aeneas (c. 1683–1689)

Henry Purcell

Dido and Aeneas is the greatest opera in the English language. The only full opera by Henry Purcell, its first documented performance dates from 1689 – the year following England's 'Glorious Revolution' – though some scholars believe it was written earlier in the decade. The libretto, by Nahum Tate (an Irish poet of meagre talent, best remembered for giving *King Lear* a happy ending), is based on Book IV of Virgil's *Aeneid*. Dido, Queen of Carthage, burns with love for the Trojan hero, Aeneas, who returns the Queen's affections but the gods – or 'sorceresses', as they appear in Tate's version – have determined that he must leave her and fulfil his destiny as the founder of the Roman race.

Despite being his only opera, and among the first in the English tradition, *Dido and Aeneas* reveals Purcell's genius for portraying his characters' emotions in music. Lively choruses and rustic dances pepper the score but it is the pervading sense of suffering, the harmonic anticipation of tragedy, that resonate most deeply. In particular, Dido's pitiful final aria is celebrated as probably the most poignant lament in musical history. Resolved to kill herself, following Aeneas' departure, the Queen of Carthage begs her handmaid to preserve her memory: 'Remember me!', she pleads above the darkly descending strings, 'Remember me, but ah! forget my fate.'

So heavy was the cost of founding the Roman race.

Recommended recording: Susan Graham, Ian Bostridge, Camilla Tilling, Felicity Palmer, David Daniels, Cécile de Boever, Paul Agnew, European Voices, Le Concert d'Astrée, Emmanuelle Haïm, Virgin Classics, 2003

2

Concerto Grosso in G Minor, 'Christmas Concerto' (c. 1685–1690)

Arcangelo Corelli

Arcangelo Corelli's oeuvre is relatively modest: 48 trio sonatas, 12 violin sonatas and 12 concerti grossi. If his output was limited, however, his influence was immense. A virtuoso violinist from a landowning family in Romagna, he developed what would become some of the most popular forms of Baroque music and established the preeminence of the violin. Bach and Handel were strongly influenced by his music, and his style was imitated by a host of lesser musicians.

A *concerto grosso* – literally, 'big concerto' – shares the musical material among a small group of soloists. Although Corelli did not invent the genre, he became its master and it is through these works, more than any others, that his name lives on.

The Concerto Grosso in G Minor is known as the 'Christmas Concerto', due to Corelli's inscription *Fatto per la notte di Natale* ('Made for the night of Christmas') on the score. Its six, short movements are, alternately, solemn and lively, with the greatest beauty reserved for the ethereal Adagio.

Recommended recording: The English Concert, Trevor Pinnock, Archiv, 1988

3

Gloria in D Major (c. 1715)

Antonio Vivaldi

Venice reached the pinnacle of her power in the 15th century. The golden years of Venetian painting – of Bellini, Giorgione, Titian and Tintoretto – were in the 16th century. Her claim to be 'The Republic of Music', however, achieved its greatest vindication between the 17th and early 18th centuries, a period bookmarked by Claudio Monteverdi composing his operas and madrigals at one end and Antonio Vivaldi producing a flood of instrumental, operatic and sacred music at the other. Although ordained as a priest when he was 25, Vivaldi spent the majority of his career working at the Ospedale della Pietà, a foundling hospital for orphans and the illegitimate children of priapic noblemen, close to St Mark's Square. There he instructed the girls in the violin and viols, worked with their renowned choir and orchestra and composed the majority of his more than 500 concertos, 100 sonatas, 50 operas and sundry sacred works.

The Gloria in D Major (one of two surviving settings of the Gloria by Vivaldi), is one of the most uplifting pieces in the choral repertory. With its famous opening octave leaps and trumpet flourishes, Vivaldi puts us in mind of one of Venice's great festivals: a feast of barges and gondolas floating down the Grand Canal. The 'Et in terra pax' is hauntingly beautiful, while the soprano duet 'Laudamus te' shimmers like a Tiepolo fresco. Always driving us forward, Vivaldi follows the celestial 'Domine Deus', for soprano and violin accompaniment, with a rustic chorus of dotted rhythms. We hear the octave leaps again at the start of the 'Quoniam tu solus sanctus' and then we are into a magnificent 'Cum sancto spiritu fuge' which concludes the piece. Written in 1715 but neglected until the great Vivaldi revival just before the Second World War, Vivaldi's Gloria captures the solemnity as well as the splendour of *La Serenissima*.

Recommended recording: Sara Mingardo, Patrizia Biccirè, Deborah York, Concerto Italiano, Champagne Ardenne Vocal Academy, Rinaldo Alessandrini, Naïve, 2007

4

Salve Regina (1707)

George Frederick Handel

George Frederick Handel was the most cosmopolitan of Baroque composers. Born in Halle, then part of Brandenburg-Prussia, in 1685 – the same year as Johann Sebastian Bach and Domenico Scarlatti – he spent four years in Italy before travelling to Hanover and, thence, to London. Handel liked London and, despite having accepted the post of Court Composer to the Elector of Hanover, decided to stay. He was rewarded with an annual pension of £200 from Queen Anne, a stipend he was able to maintain even after his short-changed former employer, Georg Ludwig, Elector of Hanover, succeeded to the English throne as George I in 1714. Just over a decade later, this German composer became a British subject. His musical maturity had, however, been reached in warmer climes.

During the first half of the 18th century, Italy was the undisputed capital of European music. 'There was no country in which a young proficient could spend his time to so much advantage,' Prince Gian Gastone de' Medici assured the

21-year-old young composer, who was then residing in Hamburg. Although initially sceptical, Handel took the Prince's advice. He visited Florence – the cradle of opera as well as the Renaissance – and, by early 1707, was making waves in Rome. Although the Papacy, suffering from characteristic reaction, had placed a ban on the performance of opera within the city, Handel and other composers were able to circumvent this injunction by staging highly theatrical oratorios and cantatas. He also composed copious church music, including his setting of the psalm *Dixit Dominus* and this prayer to the Virgin Mary.

Handel's Salve Regina was likely first performed on Trinity Sunday 1708, in the Church of Santa Maria in Montesanto, Vignanello. Scored for solo soprano, violins, organ, cello and basso continuo, it reveals the Italian influence on the young Handel, while exhibiting a beauty that is entirely the composer's own.

Recommended recording: Emma Kirkby, London Baroque, BIS, 1999

5

Brandenburg Concerto No. 4 in G Major (c. 1711–1720)

Johann Sebastian Bach

When the distinguished American biologist Lewis Thomas was asked what should be placed in the *Voyager* spacecraft (launched in 1977, to explore the outmost reaches of the Solar System), as evidence of Earth-bound civilisation, he suggested the complete works of Johann Sebastian Bach, before reflecting that this might be seen as 'boasting'. Given the tonnage of superlatives about the Cantor of St Thomas – 'Music owes as much to Bach as religion to its founder' (Robert Schumann); 'In Bach, the vital cells of music are united as the world is in God' (Gustav Mahler); 'Bach was a top harmonist geezer, which is why the jazz cats love him' (Nigel Kennedy) – it may come as a surprise to some readers to learn that for 70 years after his death in 1750, Bach all but dropped out of the musical repertoire. It was Mendelssohn who resurrected his music, in the early 19th century, and the 'Bach revival' has been going ever since.

Written between 1711 and 1720, the Brandenburg Concertos set a new standard for orchestral composition. Bach presented them to the Margrave of Brandenburg (the younger brother of King Frederick I of Prussia) in 1721, hoping that he would give him a job. On the title page, the composer penned an obsequious dedication, in which he asked the Prince not to judge too harshly 'the little talents which Heaven has given me for Music'. But the Prince did not reply. He failed to acknowledge the cultural treasure Bach had given him, did not offer to pay him and, as far as we know, never had the concertos performed. Although they have come to be known by his title, the concertos, like Bach, owe nothing to Christian Ludwig, Margrave of Brandenburg-Schwedt.

In Christian Ludwig's defence, it may have been that he did not have the forces, or the expertise, at his disposal to play the Concertos. Bach wrote the pieces for 'several instruments' but rarely the same ones: the first Brandenburg Concerto calls for a solo group of two horns, three oboes, a bassoon and violin (in addition to the small string orchestra that accompanies all six concertos); the second is for trumpet, oboe, flute and violin; the third requires nine extremely talented string soloists; the fourth a violin and two recorders; the fifth a flute and harpsichord; and the sixth, a pair of violas.

I would not be without any of these Concertos but, if forced to choose, my current favourite is the relatively neglected fourth in G, with it glorious final Fugue.

Recommended recording: Musica Antiqua Köln, Reinhard Goebel, Archiv, 1986

6

Concerto in D Minor for Oboe and Orchestra (1722)

Tomaso Albinoni

The Venetian composer Tomaso Albinoni is best known for the Adagio in G Minor for strings and organ. A rich, lachrymose lament, it has proved as popular with film directors as it has with audiences and recording companies. There is just one problem: it is not by Albinoni.

In 1958, the musicologist and Albinoni scholar, Remo Giazotto, published the Adagio, claiming to have evolved it from a fragment of Albinoni's music – six bars of melody and the basso continuo – found at the Saxon State Library in Dresden. He declined, however, to publish the original, and the continued absence of Albinoni's manuscript has led many to conclude that Giazotto (who claimed the copyright for the piece) perpetrated a profitable deception.

Poor Albinoni! Although a noted opera composer in his day, few of his operas have survived and, two centuries after his death, he was the victim of identity fraud. Fortunately, we still have many authenticated orchestral works, including his sprightly Oboe Concertos. The slow movement of his D Minor Concerto is especially moving: a simple succession of chords in the strings, the oboe high above; it makes me think of the early-morning mist lifting off the Venetian lagoon after a night of Carnival.

Recommended recording: Stefan Schilli, Stuttgart Kammerorchester, Nicol Matt, Brilliant Classics, 2005

7

Giulio Cesare in Egitto (1723–1724)

George Frederick Handel

After a slow start, English opera was soon replaced, in early 18th-century Britain, with what amounted to almost a mania for the more sophisticated Italian variety. The man tasked with satisfying this demand was Handel, who, between the presentation of *Rinaldo* in 1711 – the first Italian opera written specifically for the London stage – and his last effort, *Deidamia* in 1741, turned out more than 30 operas.

Based on Julius Caesar's 48–47 BC visit to Egypt and affair with the Egyptian Queen, Cleopatra, *Giulio Cesare* is a tale of love, revenge, desire and grief. The plot is complex and contains more than the usual number of leading characters, yet Handel rose to the challenge spectacularly. Dramatic and compelling, the score of *Giulio Cesare* is the most opulent Handel ever composed for the opera house, with an extraordinary range of characterisation and emotion. Having entered in triumph, following his victory over Pompey, Caesar, variously, displays cold fury ('Empio, dirò, tu sei'), infatuation ('Non è si vago e bello'), cunning ('Va tacito e nascosto') and the courage worthy of his name ('Al lampo dell'armi'). There are wonderful arias for Cornelia (Pompey's widow), Sesto (Pompey's son) and Ptolemy – there is, in fact, not one weak number in the entire opera – but the most sumptuous music is reserved for Cleopatra.

Written for the acclaimed Italian soprano Francesca Cuzzoni – who, famously, Handel was said to have threatened to throw out of a window if she continued to refuse to sing the opening aria of *Ottone* (1723) – the part of Cleopatra is stunningly sensual. Her aria 'V'adoro, pupille', featuring an on-stage band, is truly the stuff to melt the heart of mighty Caesar, while 'Se pietà di me', her prayer that Caesar may survive the coming battle, is hauntingly beautiful. Having defeated their enemies and proclaimed their love, Caesar and Cleopatra enter Alexandria in triumph: the orchestral accompaniment as rousing as any bourrée or hornpipe from the composer's *Water Music* suites.

Not merely Handel's finest theatrical work but the summit of Baroque opera.

Recommended recording: Marijana Mijanović, Magdalena Kožená, Anne Sofie von Otter, Charlotte Hellekant, Bejun Mehta, Alan Ewing, Les Musiciens du Louvre, Marc Minkowski, Archiv, 2002

8

Keyboard Partita No. 1 in B-flat Major (1726)

Johann Sebastian Bach

Among the wonders of Bach is how his music can be both intricate and ornate and simple and translucent at the same time. This is particularly true of his solo works. Whenever I feel jaded, or have overindulged in rich romantic fare, I return to Bach's compositions for solo keyboard – the musical equivalent of a cold glass of Alpine water: clear, pure, the source of all things.

A '*partita*' is simply a suite of music for a solo instrument. Composed between 1726 and 1731, Bach's six *partitas* for harpsichord are not only the last but arguably the best of his keyboard suites, succeeding *The English Suites* (c. 1719–1725) and *The French Suites* (1722–1725).

The First Keyboard Partita begins with a stately prelude, complete with rococo trills. The subsequent movements, contrasting yet complementary, consist of a series of 18th-century dances: an allemande, corrente, sarabande, two minuets, and, finally, a gigue. Perfectly proportioned and poised, this suite is also thrilling, with its rolling rhythms, interplay between the left and right hands and innumerable ornamentations. This is especially true of the Corrente (third movement), with its triplets, and the final Gigue, in which the left hand has to hit out the staccato melody in both the treble and the bass, while the right keeps the motor running in the centre of the keyboard.

Recommended recording: Glenn Gould, Columbia Masterworks, 1960

9

Prelude and Fugue in E-flat Major, 'St Anne' (1739)

Johann Sebastian Bach

Bach was the greatest composer for the organ and, also, the master of the fugue. His acquaintance with what Mozart called the 'king of instruments' began in his early childhood and was consummated at the prestigious St Michael's School in Lüneburg. During the course of his career, he wrote well over 200 works for the organ, and when, in 1754, a belated obituary to the composer appeared, it began with the telling heading: 'The Honourable JS Bach, world famous in organ-playing...'

The Prelude and Fugue in E-flat Major, published in 1739, is a wonderful fusion of styles: a French overture, an Italian concerto and, finally, a German fugue. The fact that there are three themes, three sections of the fugue and three flats has led many to conclude that it represents the Trinity. Writing of the rushing semiquavers in the final fugue, the theologian and organist Albert Schweitzer thought it sounded 'as if the Pentecostal wind were coming roaring from heaven'.

And St Anne? Well, she, I am afraid, had even less to do

with Bach than she did with the Trinity. Her association with the piece stems solely from the fact that, by remarkable coincidence, the start of the fugue section is almost identical to the beginning of William Croft's 1708 hymn, 'St Anne', better known by its first line, 'Oh God, our help in ages past'.

Recommended recording: Ton Koopman, Walloon Church, Amsterdam, Novalis, 1986

10

Messiah (1741)

George Frederick Handel

More often than not, it is impossible to identify a composer's masterpiece. How can we agree on Mozart's greatest work
when we cannot agree on his greatest piano concerto? Yet with
Handel – despite his 42 operas, 25 oratorios, over 40 orchestral works and much, much more – one composition shines
forth above the rest.

Messiah is associated in our minds with Christmas. Each
year, I look forward to the moment in mid-December when
I feel I can start to listen to Bach's Christmas Oratorio and
Handel's sacred masterwork with impunity. Yet while the former is, obviously, associated with the birth of Jesus, the latter was originally intended to be performed in the run-up to
Easter. Indeed, while *Messiah* anticipates and celebrates the
Nativity, at least two-thirds of it contemplate the Passion, the
Resurrection and the Ascension. This said, it is neither a narrative nor a drama. Unlike Handel's other oratorios, there are
no named characters and almost no direct speech. Rather, it
is a meditation on the life and significance of Jesus Christ –

the Messiah – with the intention of reaffirming our belief in the possibility of redemption through faith ('I know that my Redeemer liveth').

Handel gave the first performance of *Messiah* in Dublin on 13 April 1742. Having completed the work in an astonishing 24 days, he had brought it with him to Ireland, where he was due to give a series of subscription concerts. Initially, *Messiah* was not on the menu but when the public demanded more and yet more music, the composer decided to present his new oratorio at a charity concert in Passion week. The response was ecstatic. 'Words are wanting to express the exquisite Delight it afforded to the admiring crowded Audience,' sang the *Dublin Journal*, 'The Sublime, the Grand and the Tender, adapted to the most elevated, majestic and moving Words, conspired to transport and charm the ravished Heart and Ear.'

Messiah is all of these things and more. Indeed, its greatness, perhaps, lies in its ability to convey and contrast so many disparate emotions: the grave (the overture) with the hopeful ('Ev'ry valley'); the fearful ('For behold, darkness shall cover the earth') with the sprightly ('For unto us a child is born'); the terrifying ('Thou shalt break them') with all the joys of heaven (the 'Hallelujah' chorus).

Recommended recording: Emma Kirkby, Judith Nelson, Carolyn Watkinson, Paul Elliott, David Thomas, Academy of Ancient Music, Choir of Christ Church Cathedral, Oxford, Christopher Hogwood, L'Oiseau-Lyre, 1980

11

Mass in B Minor (1722–1749)

Johann Sebastian Bach

Bach, it has been said, encapsulated the spirit of Lutheranism in music. What, we may therefore ask, was he doing composing a complete setting of the Ordinary Mass in Latin, the centrepiece of the Catholic service? Not content to deprive the devil of his tunes, was he also seeking to usurp his structures?

The B Minor Mass was not, in fact, composed as a complete Mass. Bach conceived the Kyrie and Gloria – a *missa* or 'short mass' – in 1733 as part of an eventually successful effort to be appointed Court Composer to the Elector of Saxony in Dresden. Over the next 16 years, the *Missa* remained in this state while Bach produced the Second Book of *The Well-Tempered Clavier*, the *Goldberg Variations* and *The Art of the Fugue*. What prompted him, in his early sixties, to return to the *Missa* and expand it into a complete setting of the Ordinary Mass remains a mystery. One theory, which does not exclude more mundane explanations, was that Bach wished to display his mastery of a wide variety of musical styles and techniques in one great work. It is an attractive thesis, supported by the extraordinary range of complementary yet disparate fugues, chorales, choruses and solo arias that make up the work. Either way, there does seem to be a feeling of summation, even of the valedictory, about the piece. Along with Handel's *Messiah*, the Mass in B Minor constitutes the pediment atop the temple of Baroque music; a work of such glory and profundity that it can make even the irreligious contemplate the existence of angels. And yet there is a lasting irony in the fact that this most Protestant of composers should be celebrated, above all else, for a work his son catalogued as 'The Great Catholic Mass'.

Recommended recording: John Eliot Gardiner, Monteverdi Choir, English Baroque Soloists, Soli Deo Gloria, 2015

12

Music for the Royal Fireworks (1749)

George Frederick Handel

The last British monarch to lead his troops into battle was George II, at the Battle of Dettingen, in 1743 ('a happy escape rather than a great victory', as Lecky put it in his magisterial eight-volume *History of England in the Eighteenth Century*). Six years later and the same King ordered a major celebration, including fireworks, in London's Green Park, to mark the signing of the Treaty of Aix-la-Chapelle, which brought an end to the War of the Austrian Succession.

Initially, the King did not want any music but was persuaded, by the Master of the Ordnance, the Duke of Montagu, to commission some, on the condition that it be strictly martial, with 'no fiddles'. After hearing of the King's wishes, the *London Magazine* reported that Handel was busy preparing a colossal work, involving 40 trumpets, 20 French horns, 16 hautboys, 16 bassoons, eight pairs of kettle drums and a hundred cannon. Yet artistic freedom counted for something even in the 18th century, and it was thus with some degree of perturbation that Montagu wrote to a fellow courtier, on 17 March 1749, with the news that 'Handel now proposes to lessen the number of trumpets, etc. and to have violeens. I do not at all doubt but when the King hears it he will certainly be very much displeased'.

As it turned out, there was much more than 'violeens' to displease the King. In true English fashion, it rained on the night of 27 April 1749 and many of the fireworks failed to light. Worse, the great pavilion, designed by the Italian Giovanni Niccolò Servandoni, on which the musicians performed and the fireworks were lit, caught fire. A woman in the audience had her skirt set alight by a stray rocket and three soldiers were badly wounded. 'The illumination was mean,' recorded Horace Walpole, son of the late Prime Minister, 'and lighted so slowly that scarce anybody had patience to wait the finishing; and then, what contributed to the awkwardness of the whole was the right pavilion catching fire and being burnt down in the middle of the show.'

Fortunately, the music was a triumph: 'a spectacle of English pride and joy', as that Anglophile and Handelian Wolfgang Amadeus Mozart later wrote.

Recommended recording: Scottish Chamber Orchestra, Nicholas McGegan, Sony Classical, 1998

13

Magnificat (1749)

Carl Philipp Emanuel Bach

'Bach is the Father, we are the children,' declared Mozart. An unremarkable statement you might think. Well, it is until we realise that it was not Johann Sebastian Bach to whom Mozart was referring but his son, Carl Philipp Emanuel.

The fifth child and second surviving son of Johann Sebastian Bach and his first wife Maria Barbara, Carl Philipp Emanuel was the most important and prolific composer in Germany during the second half of the 18th century, eclipsing his father in fame and popularity. His oeuvre amounts to over a thousand compositions and includes keyboard sonatas and songs, symphonies and dances, trios and concertos, oratorios and cantatas. A virtuoso keyboardist, it was during his decades of service to Frederick the Great in Berlin that Bach penned his *Essay on the True Art of Playing Keyboard Instruments* – a seminal treatise which was admired by Haydn, Mozart and Beethoven.

C. P. E. Bach's Magnificat, first performed in 1749, stands midway between the Baroque style of his father and the

Classicism of the late 18th century. At times reminiscent of Vivaldi and J. S. Bach's own Magnificat, it also anticipates the melodic elegance of Haydn and Gluck. The cascading strings with adorning trumpets and tiampani in the opening movement amount to sheer musical euphoria.

Recommended recording: Venceslava Hruba-Freiberger, Barbara Bornemann, Peter Schreier, Olaf Bär, Berlin Radio Chorus, C. P. E. Bach Chamber Orchestra, Hartmut Haenchen, Berlin Classics, 1988

14

Cello Concerto No. 1 in C Major (1761–1765)

Joseph Haydn

Joseph Haydn remains perhaps the most underrated and certainly the most underexplored of the great composers. The 'Father of the Symphony', as well as of the string quartet, he wrote over a hundred of the former and 70 of the latter, as well as cantatas, masses, concertos, trios, divertimenti and dances, sonatas and songs, operas and oratorios. He even composed 32 works for the mechanical clock.

Like his great Classical contemporary Mozart, Haydn had a mischievous sense of humour. Caned when a choirboy at Vienna's St Stephen's Cathedral for cutting off another chorister's pigtail, he later indulged his puckish side by including jokes in his music. The finale of his String Quartet No. 30 in E-flat, for instance, contains a series of false endings, since the composer had, apparently, made a bet that the audience would start talking before the conclusion. (Not laugh-out-loud funny, but pretty good for 1781). Another famous joke occurs in his Symphony 'Il Distratto' ('The Distracted'). After a deliberately pompous opening, a succession of discords cause the orchestra to grind to a halt. The 'distracted' musicians have, it seems, 'forgotten' to tune their instruments – a process they now, noisily, undertake. We do not know for certain that Haydn wished to give audiences a fright in the slow movement of his Symphony No. 94, but the sudden *fortissimo* at the end of the otherwise quiet opening is certainly a 'Surprise' and another of the composer's musical pranks.

Haydn's C Major Cello Concerto No. 1 displays his wit as well as his extraordinary musicianship to the full. After a courtly opening, the first movement blends confidence with longing. The sonorous slow movement gives full expression to this sense of yearning, while the finale is gloriously effervescent: an irrepressible caper that puts the virtuosity of the soloist to the test.

Recommended recording: Jacqueline du Pré, English Chamber Orchestra, Daniel Barenboim, Warner Classics, 1967

15

Orphée et Eurydice (1762/1774)

Christoph Willibald Gluck

The appeal of Orpheus to opera composers is obvious: a classical hero who achieved fame not by the sword but through art, his music tamed the beasts and conquered death. In the years between 1600 and 1610 – the first decade of opera – no fewer than 12 works based on the Orpheus myth appeared.

Christoph Gluck is the bridge between the formal opera of French composers, such as Lully and Rameau, and the humanity of Mozart. Yet it would be a great mistake to view him as a mere causeway. Lyrical, rhythmically exciting and with a greater focus on the orchestra than his predecessors, his operas twinkle in the 18th-century firmament.

Gluck originally composed *Orphée et Eurydice* for the name-day celebrations for his employer, the Holy Roman Emperor, in 1762. Sung in Italian, with a castrato taking the male lead, it was later overhauled and substantially augmented for the Paris Opera in 1774. To conform with French tastes, Gluck added more ballet music – including the 'Dance of the Furies' and the 'Dance of the Blessed Spirits' – and transformed Orpheus from a castrato into a high tenor.

Since the opera was originally written for a feast day, the myth was altered so as to provide a happy ending (in more than one version of the original story, poor Orpheus, having lost his beloved Eurydice a second time, is ripped to shreds by maenads). Indeed, the tale of Orpheus the lover – the demi-god who refused to accept the death of his wife and travelled to the Underworld to bargain with Hades – was so inspiring that many post-antiquity writers and composers allowed him to succeed in his quest. Yet it is only in grief that Orpheus produces his greatest music, as demonstrated by the ravishing aria, 'J'ai perdu mon Eurydice'.

Recommended recording: Richard Croft, Mireille Delunsch, Marion Harousseau, Les Musiciens du Louvre, Marc Minkowski, Archiv, 2002

16

Symphony No. 48 in C Major, 'Maria Theresa' (1769)

Joseph Haydn

This was the first Haydn symphony I came to know and love. Although I would not claim it as the greatest, or even the one I reach for most frequently today, its joyful energy still has the capacity to thrill me just as when I first heard it as a seven-year-old.

Haydn did not 'invent' the symphony. He was, however, the 'father' of the genre (Mozart, among others, called him 'Papa Haydn'): the man who, over the course of more than a hundred works, reached a level of artistic and technical achievement such as could scarcely have been imagined and established the form that would serve Mozart and be developed by Beethoven.

Of Haydn's 106 symphonies, 34 have nicknames, including 'The Bear', 'The Fire', 'The Surprise', 'The Hen' and 'The Clock'. No. 48, in radiant C major, is known as 'Maria Theresa', since it was long believed to have been composed in honour of the visit of the Holy Roman Empress to Esterháza (where Haydn held the post of Court Composer) in 1773. The discovery of a manuscript of the score dating from 1769, however, proves that this was not the case. Nevertheless, the symphony has a regal feel: especially the first movement, with its horn fanfares and kettledrum rolls. The pre-eminent Haydn scholar, H. C. Robbins Landon, who unearthed a trove of forgotten pieces by the composer, describes it as 'a great and indeed germinal work'.

Recommended recording: Trevor Pinnock, The English Concert, Archiv, 1988

17

Piano Sonata No. 8 in A Minor (1778)

Wolfgang Amadeus Mozart

We do not think of Mozart's music as being autobiographical. Not only was such self-conscious subjectivity the prerogative of 19th-century Romanticism (as opposed to 18th-century Classicism), his music has a sublimity that seems hardly to belong to this world, let alone the trivialities of his own life. Yet to every rule there is an exception and the A Minor Piano Sonata may well be it.

In September 1777, the 21-year-old Mozart set off with his mother in search of employment outside his native Salzburg. It was an ill-fated quest. In Mannheim, he met the 16 or 17-year-old Aloysia Weber, a talented singer on the cusp of an operatic career, and fell in love. The composer's father, Leopold Mozart – who was relying on his gifted son to support the whole family – was horrified and ordered him to leave for Paris immediately. Although he was offered the post of organist at Versailles, Mozart failed to find a suitable position in the French capital and found the Parisians cold, without a 'modicum' of musical taste. Then his mother fell ill. On 11

June 1778, she was bled, but this ancient practice likely did more harm than good and, three weeks later, she died.

Naturally, Mozart was devastated. 'This is the saddest day of my life,' he wrote to a friend in Salzburg, beseeching him to attend his father and comfort him when the news arrived. But Leopold did not appreciate such thoughtfulness. Blaming his son for the tragedy, he reproved him for his tardiness in summoning a doctor. A few days later he wrote to Paris again, reminding Mozart how his mother had almost died giving birth to him:

> The unbreakable chain of Divine Providence preserved your mother's life when you were born, though indeed she was in very great danger...But she was fated to sacrifice herself for her son in a different way.

Although there is no documentary evidence beyond the uncharacteristically messy manuscript, it is hard to hear the anguished tonalities and hysterical rhythms of the A Minor Piano Sonata – composed just a few weeks after Maria Anna's death – and not conclude that Mozart sublimated his feelings of grief and, possibly, guilt into the work. Beginning with a cry of pain over hammering chords in the bass, the first movement maintains its tragic state even when it morphs, briefly, into C major. The F major Andante restores a sense of calm but only before launching into one of the most tortuous development sections Mozart ever wrote. The final, short, Presto is the epitome of agitated despair.

Recommended recording: Dinu Lipatti, EMI, 1951

18

Symphony No. 36 in C Major, 'Linz' (1783)

Wolfgang Amadeus Mozart

The ancient Greeks believed that artistic inspiration came from the Muses; the Romantics, from the innermost emotions of the artist. According to both theories, great art is not something that can simply be produced on demand. Well, unless you are Mozart…

In late 1783, the 27-year-old Mozart and his wife, Constanze, stopped at Linz on their way back to Vienna from Salzburg. Met at the gates of the city by a servant of the local magnate, Count Johann Joseph Anton von Thun und Hohenstein, they were escorted to the palace where the Count requested a concert. 'As I did not bring one single simphonie [sic] with me,' the composer explained in a letter to his father, 'I will have to write a new one.'

Mozart completed his Symphony No. 36, known thereafter as the 'Linz', in just five days, unveiling it on 4 November 1783. Despite the haste, it betrays no signs of rush. On the contrary, the 'Linz' marks an important development in

Mozart's symphonic writing, with a slow introduction preceding the first-movement Allegro for the first time. Although there are neither clarinets nor flutes in the symphony – presumably because there were neither clarinettists nor flautists in the Count's orchestra – the sound is nonetheless big and rich, with horns and trumpets adding weight to the oboes, bassoons and strings.

After the stately introduction, which shows the influence of Haydn, the first movement moves into an *allegro spirito*, confident and urbane. The slow-movement Siciliano (a pastoral melody in 6/8 or 12/8 time) does not tug at the heartstrings – it is a curious fact that few of Mozart's symphonic slow movements plumb the same emotional depths as their cousins do in the piano concertos – but preserves the courtly elegance, now in a minor key. A lively Minuet reintroduces a feeling of merriment, before Mozart lets loose in an inspired Presto. It is a glorious piece – one whose last movement alone would have been enough to ensure its author lasting fame – and yet if Mozart had packed his trunk differently it might never have been composed.

Recommended recording: Berlin Philharmonic, Claudio Abbado, Sony Classical, 1994

19

Piano Concerto No. 20 in D Minor (1785)

Wolfgang Amadeus Mozart

In the second half of the 18th century, when elegance and gentility were the hallmarks of taste, minor keys were considered less perfect than major ones. Of Mozart's 41 complete symphonies, only two are in minor keys (Nos. 25 and 40), while there are, similarly, only two minor piano concertos (Nos. 20 and 24) among the immortal 27. What is lacking in quantity, however, is more than made up for in depth.

The D Minor and C Minor piano concertos are equally tragic but in different ways. While the latter has all the grandeur of Lear on the heath, the former has a haunting, otherworldly quality, more akin to *Hamlet*.

It was on an appropriately cold and stormy night, on 11 February 1785, that Mozart gave the first performance of his D Minor Piano Concerto. He was at the height of his popularity and many of the leading figures in Vienna, including the Emperor, had turned out to hear Austria's premier virtuoso pianist. Leopold Mozart, who had arrived from Salzburg on the day of the concert, was alarmed to find the piece still being copied. 'Your brother did not even have time to play through the Rondo [the third movement],' he reported to Wolfgang's sister, Nannerl. The concert was, however, a triumph. As the last notes died away, the Emperor, Joseph II – infamous for, supposedly, telling the young composer that there were 'too many notes' in his opera *Die Entführung aus dem Serail* – shouted, 'Bravo Mozart!', leading the audience in applause. The next day, no less a figure than Haydn relayed to Leopold this simple truth: 'Before God and as an honest man, I tell you that your son is the greatest composer known to me either in person or in name.'

Recommended recording: Christian Zacharias, Symphonie-Orchester des Bayerischen Rundfunks, David Zinman, Warner Classics, 1989

20

Don Giovanni (1787)

Wolfgang Amadeus Mozart

It is the most terrifying opening of any opera. With two *fortissimo* D-minor chords, Mozart summons the world of the diabolical and the damned. As the strings begin to ascend and descend a rising scale, the sense of foreboding becomes overwhelming. But then, something surprising happens: the key changes from D minor to D major and a sprightly Allegro begins. Not only does the overture to *Don Giovanni* anticipate the coming opera, it epitomises Mozart's genius. No other composer explored the divide between the tragic and the comic, the capricious and the profound, the sacred and the profane, with such insight and artistry as Wolfgang Amadeus Mozart.

As its overture implies, *Don Giovanni* is the child of the two distinct operatic traditions Mozart inherited: *opera seria* (serious opera) and *opera buffa* (comic opera). Thus, while *Don Giovanni* is filled with dastardly deeds, death, duels and the fires of hell, it is also a lively comedy, with elements of slapstick. According to the tastes of the times, productions have tended to emphasise one aspect or the other. During the

19th century, for instance, the final moralising ensemble was generally cut and the opera would end with the libertine Don being dragged down to hell, since this was considered a more Romantic conclusion. Yet it is as impossible to ignore the comedy as it is the depravity. The opera opens with Don Giovanni's long-suffering servant, Leporello, grumbling about his master's behaviour. The scene is unmistakably *opera buffa*, but takes a dark twist when Donna Anna enters, pursuing the man who has just forcibly seduced her. Later, in the most dramatic scene of all, when the statue or ghost of the Commendatore appears to invite Don Giovanni to dinner, the *buffa* element is maintained by the gibbering Leporello.

At the centre of the ambivalence stands the great anti-hero himself. That Don Giovanni is a monster – a serial seducer, who commits rape and murder without scruple – is not in doubt. And yet, in Mozart's opera, created with the librettist Lorenzo da Ponte, it is possible to find ourselves siding with him, willing him to elude his pursuers. It is perhaps this moral ambiguity, this blend of light and dark, that lends *Don Giovanni* its unique fascination. The 'opera of all operas', according to the 19th-century critic, E. T. A. Hoffman, it demonstrates Mozart's understanding of complex and contradictory facets, while showcasing his mastery of ensemble, drama, harmony and melody.

Recommended recording: Ildebrando D'Arcangelo, Luca Pisaroni, Diana Damrau, Joyce DiDonato, Rolando Villazón, Mojca Erdmann, Konstantin Wolff, Vitalij Kowaljow, Mahler Chamber Orchestra, Yannick Nézet-Séguin, Deutsche Grammophon, 2011

21

Clarinet Quintet (1789)

Wolfgang Amadeus Mozart

Although the clarinet was invented around 1700, it was not until the last decades of the 18th century that it found its place in the front rank of the orchestra and as a solo instrument. That it attained such prominence and popularity owes much to Mozart.

Mozart loved the clarinet: the instrument whose mellow timbre he considered closest to the human voice. He displayed his reverence for it in his Serenade for 13 Wind Instruments, known as the 'Gran Partita' and, in 1789, added clarinets to a reorchestration of Handel's *Messiah*. The same year – the year in which the Bastille was stormed and revolution swept France – he composed his Clarinet Quintet.

As with his more famous Clarinet Concerto, Mozart wrote the Clarinet Quintet for his friend, the clarinettist Anton Stadler. That Stadler was an extraordinary virtuoso is clear from contemporary testimony: 'I have never heard the like of what you contrived with your instrument,' wrote the librettist Johann Friedrich Schink, around the time the musician made Mozart's acquaintance.

> Never should I have thought that a clarinet could be capable of imitating the human voice as it was imitated by you. Indeed, your instrument has so soft and lovely a tone that no one can resist it...

Originally composed (again, like the Clarinet Concerto) for basset clarinet – an invention of Stadler's that lowered the range of the instrument – the Clarinet Quintet is made up of four diverse movements and is among the most tender pieces Mozart produced. The slow-movement Larghetto is particularly beautiful: a caressing tune that sounds like an aria from the *Marriage of Figaro*, it is every bit as affecting as the Adagio from the Clarinet Concerto.

Recommended recording: Sabine Meyer, Wiener Streichsextett, EMI, 1988

22

The Magic Flute (1791)

Wolfgang Amadeus Mozart

When I was a teenager, I spent a lot of time trying to decide whether *The Marriage of Figaro* or *Don Giovanni* was Mozart's greatest opera (I was slightly unusual, I admit). Two master-pieces by the same artist, impossible to choose between. (Similar conundrums would include *Hamlet* or *King Lear*, *War and Peace* or *Anna Karenina*.) Then, a few years ago, I began to wonder if *The Magic Flute* did not surpass them both.

The Magic Flute is an opera of contradictions and extremes. A *singspiel* – a music drama, with dialogue between the arias, as opposed to sung recitatives – it was written to appeal to the general public and yet conceived as a 'grand opera', with large choruses, elaborate scenery and fantastic theatrical effects. A drama as well as a comedy, it combines the humour of the pantomime with lessons in Enlightenment philosophy. The whole thing can be interpreted as one great Free-Masonic alle-gory – an organisation Mozart joined in 1784 – and contains some of the highest notes in opera (the Queen of the Night reaches a top F in her famous aria, 'Der Hölle Rache kocht in meinem Herzen' – 'Hell's vengeance boils in my heart') as well as some of the lowest. Dramatic yet frivolous, popular yet profound, is this not the ultimate distillation of Mozart's genius?

Die Zauberflöte received its premiere, not in the Court Opera House, but in the Viennese suburb of Wieden, on 30 September 1791. That it was an incredible success, which gave its author justified pride, is clear from Mozart's letters to his wife. 'I have just come from the opera, which was as full as ever,' he reported on 7 October 1791:

> The duet 'Mann und Weib' ('Man and Woman') and Papageno's glockenspiel [aria] in Act I had to be repeated and also the trio of the boys in Act II. But what pleases me most is the silent applause – one can readily see how much this opera continues to grow...

The next day, he relayed a joke he had played on Emanuel Schikaneder, the opera's librettist, who was singing the part of Papageno. Having watched most of the opera from a friend's box, Mozart had slipped into the wings to satisfy an urge to play the glockenspiel that Papageno mimed on stage. Hidden from view, Mozart waited until Schikaneder was midway through a speech and then played an arpeggio. The baritone jumped. Then, when Schikaneder began to 'play' the instrument, nothing happened. Crestfallen, the singer looked as if he was about to abandon the scene when Mozart played a chord. 'Shut up!' a furious Schikaneder hissed at his collaborator, bringing the house down.

On 14 November, Mozart described how he had brought the Director of the Italian Opera at the Habsburg Court, Antonio Salieri, to hear his work. Although Salieri could be intensely jealous of his younger rival – who in his position would not be? – he was not the murderer depicted by Pushkin and Shaffer, and listened to Mozart's music with courteous attention. 'You can hardly imagine how charming they [Salieri and his singer mistress] were and how much they liked not only my music, but the libretto and everything', the composer wrote to his wife. Salieri was visibly moved and 'from the overture to the last chorus there was not a single number that did not call forth from him a "bravo!" or a "bello!"'

The Magic Flute was the greatest success of Mozart's life and should have heralded a new era of creativity, free from the oppression of financial concern. But it was not to be. Ten weeks after the first performance of *Die Zauberflöte*, he fell ill and on 5 December 1791, he died. From Wagner to Haydn, Tchaikovsky to Schubert, Rossini to Brahms, Schumann to Gounod, Chopin to Copland, Strauss to Saint-Saëns – composers of such diverse styles and views that one would hardly expect them to agree on a definition of common time – there is unanimity on one point: Mozart was the greatest musical genius that ever lived. His death on a cold December day, at the age of 35, represents a tragedy unparalleled in the history of art.

Recommended recording: Kiri Te Kanawa, Francisco Araiza, Olaf Bär, Cheryl Studer, Samuel Ramey, José van Dam, Eva Lind, Ambrosian Singers, Academy of St Martin in the Fields, Neville Marriner, Philips, 1989

23

The Creation (1797–1798)

Joseph Haydn

In order for creativity to flourish, artists must be free in body as well as imagination. For nearly 30 years Haydn worked for the fabulously rich Hungarian nobleman, Prince Nikolaus Esterházy. The Prince was a generous employer and considerable patron of the arts. He rewarded Haydn for his compositions, rebuilt his house (twice) after it burnt down and reinstated a not very talented mezzo-soprano after learning that she was the composer's mistress. In addition, he built a magnificent 400-seat opera house at his new palace of Esterháza, providing Haydn with a vehicle for all but one of his now rarely performed operas. Despite such munificence, however, Haydn's status remained that of a paid member of the Prince's household: obliged to wear the family's blue and gold livery and compelled to follow the court as it moved between Vienna, Eisenstadt and the swamp-lands of Esterháza. He was also expected to cater for his master's whims. Around 1765, Nikolaus became the proud owner of a baryton – an obscure stringed instrument, similar to a viol but with an extra set of strings at the back. Haydn was commanded to provide his employer with music for this eccentric hybrid and, over the next 15 years, turned out more than 100 baryton trios as well as numerous other works for the instrument.

The death of Nikolaus, in September 1790, freed Haydn of the baryton and, more importantly, gave him the opportunity to travel. He accepted an invitation to visit England, and thus began the most exciting and creative period of his life. Over the course of two sojourns, in 1791–92 and 1794–95, he composed his 12 great 'London Symphonies' (along with Mozart's final three, the pinnacle of the Classical form), enjoyed a passionate love affair and was universally feted. He also heard Handel's *Messiah* and *Israel in Egypt* performed by mass choirs in Westminster Abbey. According to a contemporary biographer, Haydn 'confessed that…he was struck as if he had been put back at the beginning of his studies and had known nothing up to that moment. He meditated on every note and drew from those most learned scores the essence of true musical grandeur'.

Just before Haydn left England for the last time, the impresario who had arranged his British tour, Johann Peter Salomon, presented him with a libretto for an oratorio, allegedly rejected by Handel. Taken from the Book of Genesis and Milton's *Paradise Lost*, it told the story of God's creation of the world and the brief, blissful existence of Adam and Eve in the Garden of Eden. Back in Vienna, Haydn gave the text to the Imperial Librarian, Baron Gottfried van Swieten, who saw its potential and set about turning it into a libretto for a grand oratorio in both German and English.

The Creation is an amazingly inventive work. Listen with

your eyes closed to the opening Largo – Haydn's evocation of the void before the world was formed – and you wonder if you have put on Wagner by mistake. To depict 'nothingness' in music would seem an almost impossible task, yet Haydn achieves this remarkable feat; the strings slithering in C minor before, finally, leading us out of the darkness to the triumph of C major, and 'Let there be Light!'

The rest of the work contains no less exquisite tone-painting, as well as radiant choruses, proclaiming the glory of God's handiwork. Like the 'mighty eagle' he sketches in Part II, Haydn's imagination has taken wing and, in the words of one contemporary reviewer, it is hard to believe 'that the human bellows, the gut of sheep and the skin of calves could produce such miracles.'

Recommended recording: Gundula Janowitz, Christa Ludwig, Fritz Wunderlich, Dietrich Fischer-Dieskau, Walter Berry, Vienna Singverein, Berlin Philharmonic, Herbert von Karajan, Deutsche Grammophon, 1966–1969

24

Missa in Angustiis, 'Nelson Mass' (1798)

Joseph Haydn

The title Haydn originally gave his D Minor Mass was *Missa in Angustiis* – a 'Mass for Troubled Times'. The times were certainly troubled. Napoleon had won four major battles against Austria in less than a year and, in May, had struck against Britain's trade routes by invading Egypt. At the same time, Haydn was in poor health – exhausted after composing *The Creation* – and his new employer, Nikolaus II of Esterházy, was cutting back on court expenditure. There are no woodwind in the *Missa in Angustiis*. An artistic statement by the composer? Not really. Nikolaus had sacked his wind players earlier in the year, forcing Haydn to use an organ instead.

What the composer did not know was that on 1 August 1798, Vice Admiral Horatio Nelson, with almost reckless bravery, had destroyed the French Fleet at the Battle of the Nile. The French Revolutionary army was stranded in Egypt and Napoleon, for the first but not the last time, abandoned his troops to save his own career. The news of the victory is believed to have arrived in Vienna just before the first performance of the Mass which, shortly afterwards, was rechristened 'The Lord Nelson Mass'. Two years later, Nelson himself, along with his mistress, Lady Hamilton, visited Esterháza and may well have heard the piece.

It is, of course, *ex post facto* but it is hard not to imagine the British broadsides as the timpani reverberate through the Kyrie (*Kyrie eléison* – 'Lord, have mercy' – the first prayer of the Mass ordinary), just as it is tempting to think of the jubilant Gloria as in some way anticipatory of the great victory, many miles away, on troubled waters.

Recommended recording: Bach-Collegium Stuttgart, Oregon Bach Festival Chorus, Helmuth Rilling, Hänssler Classic, 2006

25

Violin Sonata No. 9 in A Major, 'Kreutzer' (1803)

Ludwig van Beethoven

We think of Beethoven as the quintessential Romantic artist: a lonely misanthrope, isolated from his fellow men by his disability and his genius. His A Major Violin Sonata, known as the 'Kreutzer', however, shows how the young composer could be inspired by the company and artistry of others.

George Augustus Polgreen Bridgetower was a virtuoso violinist who had made his concert debut at the age of ten. The son of a West Indian father and Austro-German mother, he made his musical name in London, where he was marketed as the 'son of an African Prince' and enjoyed the patronage of the Prince of Wales. In 1802 he travelled to the continent and, in the spring of the following year, was introduced to Vienna's leading young composer. Beethoven was taken with Bridgetower – 'a very capable virtuoso who has a complete command of his instrument' – and soon began to compose a new violin sonata which the two men could perform together.

Although Beethoven resurrected a discarded finale for the third movement, the composition of the first two movements went to the wire. Beethoven's pupil, Ferdinand Ries, recalled being roused on the morning of the concert and instructed to copy out the violin part from the manuscript. Ries set to it but only had time to transcribe the first movement, forcing Bridgetower – who, in any case, was playing the sonata for the first time – to share Beethoven's score for the Andante. Despite this, the concert was a triumph. The slow movement was encored twice and, when Bridgetower added a virtuosic flourish, the composer leapt up from the keyboard and exclaimed, 'Once more, my dear fellow!' Naturally, Beethoven dedicated the sonata to 'the great madman', as he affectionately referred to Bridgetower, but the two men then quarrelled and the piece was rededicated to the French violinist, Rodolphe Kreutzer, who did not understand it and never played it.

The 'Kreutzer' Sonata, the ninth of Beethoven's ten complete violin sonatas, is far more ambitious and emotional than its predecessors. Coursing with nervous energy, the first movement is part duel, part erotic coupling, between the violin and piano. So passionate, indeed, is this movement that Tolstoy chose it as the device by which to unlock the murderous jealousy of the protagonist in his 1889 novella, named after the sonata:

'How can the first Presto be played in a drawing-room among ladies in low-necked dresses?' demands Pozdnyshev. 'Such things should only be played on certain important significant occasions... Otherwise an awakening of energy and feeling unsuited both to the time and the place, to which no outlet is given, cannot but act harmfully.'

Handle with care.

Recommended recording: Itzhak Perlman, Vladimir Ashkenazy, Decca, 1973

26

Piano Concerto No. 5 in E-flat, 'Emperor' (1809–1811)

Ludwig van Beethoven

The nickname 'Emperor' for Beethoven's fifth and final piano concerto is inappropriate in at least three ways: it was coined not by the composer but, most likely, as a marketing gimmick by the English publisher of the piece; it was begun in 1809, when Vienna was under siege from the Emperor Napoleon, whose name the composer had famously removed from the title page of his Third Symphony after the Corsican General had proclaimed himself Emperor in May 1804; and Beethoven had scant affection for the Habsburg Emperor Francis I – no longer Holy Roman Emperor, since Napoleon had dissolved that cumbersome anachronism in 1806, but merely Emperor of Austria.

And yet, Beethoven's E-flat Piano Concerto is the 'Emperor' of piano concertos. Bold and imperious in its opening – with cadenza-like runs up and down the keyboard before a lavish orchestral introduction – the first movement displays the full force and majesty of the composer's 'Heroic' period. The second movement, by contrast, is the quintessence of calm: a dream-like Adagio of gentle beauty. The concerto concludes with a bravura Rondo of irrepressible exuberance.

Recommended recording: Leif Ove Andsnes, Mahler Chamber Orchestra, Sony Classical, 2014

27

Symphony No. 7 in A Major (1811–1812)

Ludwig van Beethoven

The composer Carl Maria von Weber considered it evidence that Beethoven had gone mad. The conductor Thomas Beecham described the last movement as like 'a lot of yaks jumping about'. But for Wagner it was the 'apotheosis of the dance', and Beethoven viewed it as one of his 'best works'.

Beethoven's Seventh Symphony is an obsessional work, since to hear it is to become obsessed – if not possessed – by its obsessive, repetitive, rhythmic insistence. Unlike its predecessor, 'The Pastoral', the Seventh does not rely on obvious melodic lines that develop during the course of each movement. Indeed, it may be Beethoven's least melodic symphony. Where it derives its astonishing intensity is from the dotted rhythms that Beethoven reiterates with daring persistence. For the composer's biographer, Jan Swafford, the Seventh has the character of a bacchanale, and there is, indeed, something both frenzied and mesmerising about it.

The second movement, in particular, has fascinated and

delighted audiences ever since it was encored at the premiere in 1812. Its doleful rhythm – so consistent as to be almost mundane – and mournful tune have led some conductors to interpret it as a funeral march. Yet Beethoven marked it *allegretto* (a little lively), not *marcia funebre*, as he did in his 'Eroica' Symphony and the final movement of his A-flat Piano Sonata. The second movement is, therefore, another dance – a melancholy dance admittedly – and only a slow movement in the sense that it is literally slower than the other three. After a capering Scherzo, in which the sections of the orchestra seem to be engaged in their own, interweaving dance, we come to Beecham's 'yaks' or, alternatively, one of the most exciting finales in symphonic history.

Recommended recording: Carlos Kleiber, Vienna Philharmonic, Deutsche Grammophon, 1976

28

The Barber of Seville (1816)

Gioachino Rossini

Imagine attaining such artistic, critical and financial success that you are able to retire while still in your thirties. Gioachino Rossini wrote 39 operas, established a reputation as the master of *opera buffa* (comic opera), and then, at the age of 37, stopped. Over the next quarter of a century, he composed little music and no opera. He did, however, move to Paris, where he enjoyed *la grande vie*, entertaining in his salon, eating in the best restaurants and having the steak dish 'Tournedos Rossini' named after him. (He once said that there were only three occasions on which he had cried in his life: once when his first opera failed; once when he heard Paganini play the violin; and once when, 'with a boating party, a truffled turkey fell into the water'.)

The Barber of Seville is Rossini's masterpiece. A comic opera, written when he was just 24, it brims with catchy tunes, superb ensembles and helter-skelter tempi. The libretto is taken from the first part of the *Figaro Trilogy* by Pierre Beaumarchais and is, thus, the prequel to the tale told in Mozart's *Marriage of*

Figaro. In Rossini's opera, Count Almaviva has come to Seville to court his future wife, Rosina. Unfortunately, Rosina is effectively a prisoner in the house of her guardian, Dr Bartolo, who wants to marry her. Fortunately, the local barber, Figaro, specialises in fixing other people's problems and offers Almaviva his assistance. Take a ladder, a variety of ludicrous disguises and a well-placed bribe and the lovers are soon running rings round the curmudgeonly doctor.

Done well on stage, it is laugh-out-loud funny but the joy of the piece can be conveyed through the music alone. As the man who would succeed Rossini as the undisputed master of Italian opera, Giuseppe Verdi, later put it:

> For the abundance of true musical ideas, for its comic verve and the accuracy of its declamation, [*The Barber of Seville*] is the most beautiful *opera buffa* there is.

Recommended recording: Roberto Servile, Sonia Ganassi, Ramon Vargas, Angelo Romero, Franco de Grandis, Hungarian Radio Chorus, Failoni Chamber Orchestra, Will Humburg, Naxos, 1992

29

Piano Sonata No. 32 in C Minor (1822)

Ludwig van Beethoven

Beethoven's piano sonatas constitute the most extraordinary collection of solo piano pieces in music: the 'New Testament', in Hans von Bülow's memorable phrase, following the 'Old Testament' of Bach's *Well-Tempered Clavier*. Over the course of these 32 works, written between 1795 and 1822, it is possible to chart the course of Beethoven's artistic development as he moved from the Classicism of Mozart and Haydn, through the storm and stress of his 'middle period', to an introspection and transcendence that leave us in ecstatic bewilderment.

Beethoven's final piano sonata (No. 32, Op. 111) is in C minor, the same fateful key as his Fifth Symphony, *Coriolan* Overture and Third Piano Concerto. Beginning with a majestic, slow introduction, reminiscent of the opening of his 'Pathétique' Sonata (also in C minor), the first movement tumbles into a tempestuous *allegro con brio ed appassionato*: violent and assertive. There is a brief respite with the arrival of the gentle, second theme in A-flat but this is a mere pause and, soon, we are off again on our turbulent journey. The second, final movement is one of the most innovative movements Beethoven ever composed. An arietta (a short song) in translucent C major, its subsequent variations become so rhythmically complex and syncopated that at times it seems as if Beethoven had invented jazz or ragtime, 70 years before Scott Joplin.

In Thomas Mann's *Doktor Faustus* (1947), the musicologist Wendell Kretschmar argues that this final movement represents 'an end without any return...not only [of] this one in C minor but [of] the sonata in general as a species, as a traditional art form'. Not only is it impossible to imagine a third movement following the Arietta but a further sonata by the composer seems inconceivable. Beethoven had taken the genre to its furthest limits: a truth which is revealed by the fact that, while a few composers dabbled in the genre (most notably Chopin), the vast majority (including Chopin) were forced, hereafter, to search for new means of expression on the keyboard. Appraising the very end of the sonata – the last time we hear the Arietta theme – Mann's musicologist rises to the level of poetry:

> It is the most moving, consolatory [and] reconciling thing in the world. It is like having one's hair or cheek stroked, lovingly, understandingly, like a deep and silent farewell look. It blesses the listener with overpowering humanity and lies in parting so gently on the hearer's heart as an eternal valediction that it brings tears to the eyes.

Recommended recording: Daniel Barenboim, Deutsche Grammophon, 1984

30

Nacht und Träume (c.1822)

Franz Schubert

Franz Schubert was the greatest songwriter the world has ever known. He was also one of the most prolific: composing some 600 *lieder* over the course of his brief life.

'Nacht und Träume' ('Night and Dreams') conflates two poems by Matthäus von Collin, a friend of the composer's. Over incredibly long melodic lines, requiring the most rigorous breath control, and marked *pianissimo* throughout, the singer laments the coming of dawn, which ends those dreams that fill 'the silent hearts of men': 'Come back, holy night! / Fair dreams, return!'

Melancholy yet love-filled, this song of gentle yearning seems to belong to the same world as the nocturnal landscapes of the painter Caspar David Friedrich.

Recommended recording: Ian Bostridge, Julius Drake, Warner Classics, 1996

31

Fantasy in C Major, 'Wanderer Fantasy' (1822)

Franz Schubert

With many of Schubert's masterpieces cast in the same tragic-romantic mould as 'Nacht und Träume' – the 'Unfinished' Symphony, *Winterreise* and *Schwanengesang*, to name but three – it would be easy to imagine the young composer as a perpetual depressive. In fact, although Schubert would become increasingly melancholic as his health deteriorated, he could also be boisterous, not to say rowdy. He began composing at six o'clock every morning but, in the evenings, could be found singing and carousing with friends. Frequently, he over-did it. There is more than one anecdote about the composer becoming so drunk as to have to be carried home, as well as several references to what appears to have been a voracious sexual appetite. His friends thought he had a split personality and, indeed, he may have suffered from cyclothymia (a mild form of manic depression). 'His body, strong as it was, succumbed to the cleavage in his – I would like to say souls,' recalled the poet and painter Josef Kenner. 'The one pressed heavenwards and the other wallowed in slime.' Another friend put it less luridly: 'Schubert had, so to speak, a double nature, the Viennese gaiety being interwoven with and ennobled by a trait of deep melancholy. Inwardly a poet and outwardly a kind of hedonist.'

At first glance, the *Wanderer Fantasy* – so named because it constitutes a four-movement set of variations on the theme from his song *Der Wanderer* – seems to belong to the latter side of the composer's personality. Composed in 'happy' C major, its great chords are confident and rambunctious – the music of the youth who announced his arrival at a New Year's party by throwing stones at the window, shattering the glass. But listen again and one starts to wonder: *can all this violence – a sort of pianistic head-banging – be the work of a happy man?* Certainly, the *Wanderer Fantasy* is by far the most difficult and virtuosic piano piece Schubert ever composed. A huge challenge for pianists, requiring the greatest dexterity and energy, its technical demands, it appears, surpassed even those of its author. 'Once when Schubert was playing the *Fantasy*,' recalled the painter Leopold Kupelwieser, 'and got stuck in the last movement, he sprang up from his seat with the words: "Let the devil play the stuff!"'

Recommended recording: Sviatoslav Richter, Warner Classics, 1963

32

Symphony No. 9 in D Minor (1822–1824)

Ludwig van Beethoven

Beethoven went deaf. This fact is so well known that it is worth taking a moment to consider, lest familiarity breeds insouciance.

It was in the summer of 1798, when he was 27, that Beethoven first noticed problems with his hearing. According to the composer's own account, a towering rage brought on a fit, which caused him to collapse on the floor. When he got up, he could not hear. This deafness passed but Beethoven's hearing would never be the same. Plagued with a cacophony of roaring, raging, ringing sounds, he despaired as doctor after doctor failed to provide a cure. 'I lead a miserable life,' he wrote to his friend Franz Wegeler in July 1801:

> For almost two years I have ceased to attend any social functions, just because I find it impossible to say to people: I am deaf…in the theatre I have to place myself quite close to the orchestra in order to understand what the actor is saying and

at a distance I cannot hear the high notes of instruments or voices.

One year later, in a famous unsent letter to his brothers, written during his stay at the village of Heiligenstadt, the composer confessed to having contemplated suicide but had held back for the sake of his art: 'It seemed impossible to me to leave this world before I had produced all that I felt capable of producing and so I prolonged this wretched existence.' Over the next two decades, Beethoven would produce some of the greatest masterpieces in western art. His creativity flourished but his body deteriorated. By 1814, his piano playing had become an embarrassment ('In the *forte* passages the poor deaf man pounded on the keys until the strings jangled,' recalled the violinist and composer Louis Spohr) and by 1818 he was forced to rely on conversation books to communicate. That he went on to compose the *Missa Solemnis*, his last piano sonatas, the late string quartets and the Ninth Symphony, despite this most egregious of disabilities, is testament not only to an extraordinary resilience of spirit but a genius of unfathomable proportions.

Beethoven had expressed a desire to set Schiller's 'An die Freude' ('Ode to Joy') as early as 1790. It was not, however, until 1822, three years after he had received a symphonic commission from the London Philharmonic Society, that he began to sketch the tune that would accompany Schiller's verses and form the crux of the unprecedented choral finale to his new symphony. The theme is simple and declamatory: a melody that would stay in the memory and personify Schiller's paean to brotherly joy. This was to be the anthem of Beethoven's creed, music on the model of French Revolutionary songs and Haydn's 'God save the Emperor Francis', that would proclaim the fellowship of man. This is the end-point: the summation not only of the symphony but of Beethoven's philosophy. But we have to get there.

The first movement of the Ninth Symphony begins with the steady build-up of indistinct tones: a mysterious layering of instruments and harmonies that sounds like the gathering of cosmic dust before the expansion of the universe. Then, bang! The world is born, not with the radiance of Haydn's C Major 'Let There be Light!', but with overwhelming portent, if not outright catastrophe. The first movement stamps and rages for a quarter of an hour – considerably the longest and most complex of Beethoven's opening movements – before concluding with a funeral march of cataclysmic despair. The outlook is bleak indeed and is hardly improved by the Scherzo, whose relentless, driving rhythm and accompanying timpani blows seem like the expression of neat strife. Only in the slow-movement, *adagio molto e cantabile* (*very* slow and with a singing quality), do we find tranquillity: a theme and variations of surpassing beauty.

The famous, final movement opens with a return to the chaos of the Allegro. After Beethoven has recapitulated the central ideas of the earlier movements, the 'Joy' theme emerges: soft and tentative at first, then striding forth in resplendent glory. After a repeat of the opening chaos motif – what Wagner called the 'terror fanfare' – the baritone enters with the injunction: '*O Freunde, nicht diese Töne! Sondern laßt uns angenehmere anstimmen, und freudenvollere*' ('Oh friends, not these sounds! Let us instead strike up more pleasing and more joyful ones!'). 'Joy!' he cries. 'Joy! Joy!', the basses and tenors echo. The baritone sings the full 'Joy' theme and enjoins the choir to follow suit:

> Joy, thou lovely god-engendered
> Daughter of Elysium,
> Drunk with fire we enter,
> Heavenly one, thy holy shrine!
> Thy magic reunites
> What fashion has broken apart
> All men shall become brothers
> Where thy gentle wing abides.

The second verse, given to the quartet of soloists, begins:

> Whoever has had the great success to be a friend to a friend,
> He who has won a sweet wife,
> Join our jubilation!

(Poignant lines for the composer whose deafness was such a barrier to companionship and who, despite longing for love, never married.)

After the 'Joy' theme has appeared in the guise of a military march, been subjected to a lusty fugue and repeated *fortissimo* by the whole choir, Beethoven embarks on a choral fugue that adds a transcendental element to all this earth-bound joy:

> Be embraced, you millions!
> This kiss for all the world!
> Brothers! Over the starry canopy
> A loving Father must dwell.

The symphony ends in Bacchic frenzy. With cymbals clashing, piccolo piping and triangle ringing, the choir gives way to the delirious rapture that, so it proclaims, is the inheritance of all humanity. It is a thrilling conclusion to what is, in my far from unique opinion, the greatest symphony ever written. But there was sadness as well as joy at the premiere at the Theater am Kärntnertor on 7 May 1824. Although functionally deaf, Beethoven insisted on 'conducting' his new work and, in the words of one musician, 'threw himself back and forth like a madman', flailing his arms 'as if he wanted to play all the instruments and sing all the chorus parts'. Fortunately the official conductor, Michael Umlauf, had witnessed the havoc that had ensued when Beethoven had tried to conduct a dress rehearsal of his opera, *Fidelio*, and told the orchestra to ignore the composer. Despite a lack of rehearsal, the performance went without a hitch and, following the last cymbal clash, the audience broke into delirious applause. But Beethoven did not turn. Gently, the alto, Caroline Unger, walked over and by tugging at his sleeve, alerted him to the acclaim he could now see but could not hear.

Recommended recording: Karita Mattila, Violeta Urmana, Thomas Moser, Thomas Quasthoff, Eric Ericson Chamber Choir, Swedish Chamber Choir, Berlin Philharmonic, Claudio Abbado, Deutsche Grammophon, 2000

33

String Quartet No. 13 in A Minor, 'Rosamunde' (1824)

Franz Schubert

Schubert composed his String Quartet in A Minor, the 'Rosamunde', as well as its more famous sibling, 'Death and the Maiden', between February and March 1824, in what was probably the bleakest period of his life. Having contracted syphilis – then a fatal disease – sometime during the winter of 1822–1823, he had been in dreadful health for over a year, with painful swellings, a burning rash and the loss of most of his hair.

In addition to these ailments, he was in financial straits and his latest attempts to stage an opera had ended in failure. (It is one of the great perplexities that Schubert, the supreme songwriter, never produced a successful opera, despite 15 attempts.) Writing to a friend in the month he completed these two minor quartets, he asked him to imagine a man:

> Whose health will never be right again and who in sheer despair over this makes everything thing worse and worse…

imagine a man, I say, whose most brilliant hopes have perished, to whom the felicity of love and friendship have nothing to offer but pain… 'My peace is gone [he quotes from Goethe's Faust], my heart is sore, I shall find it never and nevermore.'

It is, of course, far from the case that works of art necessarily reflect the state of the artist at the time of their creation. Schubert's Octet – which belongs to the same period as 'Rosamunde' and 'Death and the Maiden' – is among the most glowingly 'happy' pieces he ever wrote. Yet the two minor quartets do seem redolent of the desperate situation in which the composer found himself, only a few months into his 27th year.

Although emanating from the same place, the A Minor and D Minor quartets offer contrasting responses. While the latter – known as 'Death and the Maiden' on account of the haunting theme from the second movement, taken from Schubert's song of the same name – displays an often violent despair, the former is more contemplative. With each movement beginning *pianissimo*, Schubert seems to be weeping for what he has lost, the third-movement Minuet recalling his setting of Schiller's lines, 'Beauteous world, where art thou? Return again, fair springtime of Nature'. The theme from the Andante is borrowed from his incidental music for the play *Rosamunde*, hence its name. It is a melody of such tender beauty that Schubert could not resist recycling it again in his B-flat Major Impromptu.

Recommended recording: Artemis Quartet, Erato, 2009

34

String Quartet No. 15 in A Minor (1825)

Ludwig van Beethoven

For many, Beethoven's late string quartets constitute the summit of 'classical' music, if not of all art. Written at the end of his life, when he was functionally deaf, these five works of extraordinary originality and complexity seem to penetrate the very essence of the human condition, while taking the Classical form to it furthest limits. 'After this, what is left for us to write?' enquired Schubert after hearing Beethoven's Quartet in C-sharp Minor, a few days before his death.

The String Quartet No. 15 in A Minor, like the others in this series, deals in extreme contrasts: light versus dark, loud versus soft, life versus languor. Beethoven started working on it in the early months of 1825 but in April fell seriously ill. His bowels, which had troubled him for years, had become inflamed and soon he was confined to bed. The doctor ordered him to abstain from wine, coffee, spirits and spices and, when the weather was warmer, Beethoven travelled to the spa town of Baden to convalesce. By 13 May, he thought that he might be well enough to try a little 'white wine with water' but confessed that he had been coughing up 'rather a lot of blood' and was still very weak.

Whether or not Beethoven feared that the end was near, his heart-felt gratitude at his recovery is expressed in the A Minor String Quartet: the hymn-like slow movement bearing the title '*Heiliger Dankgesang eines Genesenen an die Gottheit ...*' ('Holy song of thanksgiving of a convalescent to the Deity'). The soft, canon-like opening of this Adagio feels like an awakening after a terrible ordeal. As the chorale unfolds, we feel the pain leave our bodies. We are at peace: suspended, in gentle harmony, between consciousness and unconsciousness. As the music starts to breathe, with cautious crescendos, the sweetness of relief spreads from our core to the extremities. We are getting better and, with a key change to D major, comes a renewed sense of life. But it is too soon. Our recovery will take time and, after a repetition of this dance-like flash (which Beethoven marked '*Neue Kraft fühlend*' ('Feeling of new strength')), we sink back into our beds. The last few minutes of this movement comprise some of the most love-filled, numinous music ever written. It is almost as if, after a lifetime of struggle, deprivation and loneliness, Beethoven has finally accepted his fate and, in acceptance, found transcendence and peace.

Recommended recording: The Alban Berg Quartett, EMI, 1984

35

Overture to A Midsummer Night's Dream (1826)

Felix Mendelssohn

Felix Mendelssohn was the greatest child prodigy since Mozart. The son of a banker and grandson of the great German-Jewish philosopher, Moses Mendelssohn, he excelled at both the piano and the violin and, by the age of 15, had composed 13 string symphonies, one full symphony, five concertos, four operas, several psalm settings, six piano sonatas, two violin sonatas and numerous fugues and songs. 'A genius can curl the bristles of a pig,' declared Mendelssohn's teacher, the rough-speaking Carl Friedrich Zelter and, in October 1821, pupil and pedagogue set out to test this theory on Germany's most celebrated artist.

Johann Wolfgang von Goethe, venerated, across Europe, as the author of *The Sorrows of Young Werther* and *Faust*, was not always reliable when it came to musical judgements. Although he adored Mozart, he was equivocal about Beethoven and did not even bother to reply to a missive from Schubert, containing songs set to the poet's verse. His friendship with Zelter ensured Mendelssohn an audience, but the great man was determined to test the latest wunderkind. 'I played for Goethe for over two hours, in part fugues by Bach and in part I improvised,' reported the 12-year-old Felix to his father. 'The whole company was thunderstruck,' recalled Ludwig Rellstab, the critic who first applied the epithet 'Moonlight' to Beethoven's C-sharp Minor Piano Sonata. Having repeated a song his teacher had played on the piano, Mendelssohn plunged into the wildest Allegro, the gentle melody transformed, Rellstab said, 'into a surging figure which he took first in the bass, then in the soprano voice, developing it with lovely contrasts – in short…a torrential fantasia that poured out like liquid fire.'

After recreating the overture to Mozart's *Marriage of Figaro* on the piano and sight-reading an original manuscript of Beethoven's, Mendelssohn performed one of his own piano quartets, accompanied by three of Weimar's court musicians. Before the performance, Zelter – who considered it his duty to prevent his pupil from getting too big for his boots – asked the audience to be sparing in their praise. Once Mendelssohn had left the room, however, the 'Sun of Weimar' gave his verdict:

It is true that these days musical prodigies are not such a great rarity, particularly in their technical facility. Yet what this little man is capable of in improvisation and in sight-reading borders on the miraculous. I would not have thought it possible in one so young.

Mendelssohn reached musical maturity with his Octet – a jewel of a piece, composed when he was just 16. Less than a year later, in a letter to his sister Fanny (also a gifted pianist and composer), he announced his intention to undertake a work of 'immense boldness', to dare 'to dream a *Midsummer Night's Dream*'.

Mendelssohn's overture to *A Midsummer Night's Dream*, is a remarkable work and not just because it was written by a 17-year-old. After three rising chords in the wind, the strings begin to vibrate *pianissimo*, conjuring an image of fairies congregating in a wooded glade. There is clearly magic in the air: an enchantment which is, temporarily, broken when the full orchestra bursts forth to proclaim the majesty of the court of Athens. The lovers are represented by the sumptuous second theme, while the entry of the craftsmen players is denoted by orchestral stomping. The overture ends as it started: the fairies disbanding, their night's mischief complete, and the woodwind repeating the chords that cast the original spell.

Recommended recording: Seiji Ozawa, Boston Symphony Orchestra, Deutsche Grammophon, 1992

36

Fantasy in F Minor (1828)

Franz Schubert

It is a cruel irony that Schubert achieved unambiguous public success just as the sands were running out. On 26 March 1828 – the first anniversary of Beethoven's death – the 31-year-old composer staged the one and only public concert dedicated entirely to his own work during his lifetime. The event was hosted by the Gesellschaft der Musikfreunde ('Society of Friends of Music in Vienna') and consisted of a performance of the first movement of his G Major String Quartet, several songs – including the specially composed 'Auf dem Strom' – and his E-flat Piano Trio. The house was full and appreciative. 'Enormous applause', recalled the composer's friend, Eduard von Bauernfeld, who also reported that Schubert had netted some 800 florins from ticket sales. Flush with cash, the composer insisted on taking his friends to hear the Italian violin wizard Niccolò Paganini, currently visiting Vienna. 'I have already heard him once,' he told Bauernfeld. 'I tell you, we shall never see the fellow's like again! And I have stacks of money now, so come on!'

Over the next seven months, Schubert would continue to churn out great works at an astonishing rate. He completed his Mass in E-flat in June 1828 and, between September and the end of October, composed his String Quintet in C, his last three piano sonatas and the 14 songs that would become known as *Schwanengesang* ('Swansong'). His artistry was in the ascent but his body was giving way. By the autumn he was suffering regular bouts of giddiness, headaches and nausea and, in November, having moved into his brother's house, in the Viennese suburb of Wieden, he took to his bed with a fever. Schubert died on 19 November 1828, at the tragically early age of 31. The immediate cause of his death remains a matter of dispute but it is possible that he contracted typhus while also suffering from tertiary syphilis.

The F Minor Fantasy for piano duet is among the most emotionally charged pieces Schubert ever wrote. Composed between January and March 1828, it is illustrative, like the *Wanderer Fantasy* before it, of Schubert's desire to fuse supposedly separate movements into a continuous whole. There, however, the comparison ends. For while the *Wanderer Fantasy* begins in the most assertive, grandiose manner, the F Minor Fantasy opens with a heart-rending theme, akin to musical weeping. Over the next 18 minutes, Schubert displays, by turns, defiance, whimsy, rage, rustic vitality and restrained nostalgia. As an epitaph for the composer's brief life, it could hardly be bettered.

Recommended recording: Murray Perahia, Radu Lupu, Sony Classical, 1984

37

Symphonie fantastique (1830)

Hector Berlioz

We have all been there. There has been a point in all our lives
when we have developed a crush on someone we do not know.
On Tuesday 11 September 1827, the 23-year-old Hector
Berlioz went to see a troupe of English players perform *Hamlet*
at the Place de l'Odéon in Paris. A highly sensitive young man
(the mere announcement that his favourite Gluck opera was
being performed was enough to give him a nosebleed), he fell
madly in love with the actress playing Ophelia, Harriet Smithson. 'The impression made on my heart and mind by her
extraordinary talent, nay her dramatic genius, was equalled
only by the havoc wrought in me by the poet she so nobly
interpreted.' He wrote to her – fine. He continued to write to
her after she sent a message rejecting his love – less fine. He
rented an apartment opposite hers and observed her movements – *Gendarme*!

Despite her refusal to meet him, Berlioz's passion for Harriet continued to burn for nearly three years. 'My heart is a
furnace of raging fire,' he wrote to a friend in August 1829,

after the object of his desire had departed for Amsterdam. 'At times the fire appears to abate, then a gust of wind, a fresh flaring up, the cry of trees engulfed in the flames, reveal its terrible power of devastation.' Having suffered a nervous collapse, during which he could hardly walk or dress himself for trembling, he turned to opium to calm his nerves. And yet, his creative energy was not stilled but led him, with increasing determination, towards a grand symphony that would express his 'infernal passion' and demonstrate his genius to the world. In March 1830, he began work and, six weeks later, the *Symphonie fantastique* was born.

Thanks to Berlioz's programme notes, we have a detailed knowledge of the tale he wished to tell. The first movement reveals an artist – a 'hero you will have no difficulty in recognising', as the composer wrote to a friend – who falls in love with a young woman who conforms to the 'ideal of beauty and fascination that his heart has so long invoked'. The 'love melody' is an *idée fixe*: a musical obsession, which haunts the artist throughout the piece. Despite the distraction of a ball – represented by a waltz in the second movement – or the idyll of the countryside – depicted in the third – the artist cannot shake it. It then becomes deeply surreal. Convinced that his love is not reciprocated, the hero takes an overdose of opium and imagines that he has murdered his beloved. The fourth movement constitutes a 'march to the scaffold', where the unfortunate artist, in a double out-of-body experience, is forced to witness his own execution.

It seems as if the symphony has concluded: the fury of the brass proclaiming the demise not only of the hero but of Berlioz's drug-fuelled musical journey. But it has not finished. In a fifth movement, Berlioz leads us into the realm of the gothic and the truly bizarre. The scene is a witches' sabbath. The beloved appears and takes part in her murderer's funeral. Bells toll, demons and sorcerers prostrate themselves and the company whirl round to the fateful tones of the Dies irae ('Day of Wrath'), soon corrupted into a devilish burlesque. The nightmare ends with a tumult of trombones and trumpets.

There is much more that can be said about the *Symphonie fantastique* but perhaps the most remarkable fact is its date: 1830 – a mere three years after Beethoven's death. Such vivid programme music, such unbridled drama and subjectivity, such mastery of large-scale forces and narrative: these were the aspirations of Mussorgsky and other late-19th- and even early-20th-century composers. And yet, at the time of its composition, Mussorgsky had not even been born. Berlioz's obsession with Harriet Smithson – which, not long after the premiere of the symphony, led to an ultimately unhappy marriage – helped spawn a work that was truly ahead of its time; a piece which may, paradoxically, be regarded as both the birth and summit of French musical Romanticism.

Recommended recording: Charles Munch, Boston Symphony Orchestra, RCA Red Seal, 1962

38

Norma (1831)

Vincenzo Bellini

If Vincenzo Bellini had not died at the pitifully early age of 33, it is likely that we would speak of him in the same, venerated breath as Verdi. In his brief life, he wrote ten operas and, by the time of his death, had reached a level of musical maturity far beyond his years.

It was *Il Pirata*, the opera Bellini unveiled at La Scala in October 1847, that catapulted him to fame at the tender age of 25. Another commission from the Milanese opera house followed and soon impresarios were falling over themselves to secure the young man's services. In 1830, he was paid the astonishing sum of 10,000 francs for *La Sonnambula* – the highest fee for a single opera to date and double what Rossini had been awarded for *Semiramide*. The same year, he signed a contract with La Scala for two operas for the 1831–32 season, the first of which was to be *Norma*.

As usual, Bellini insisted on working with the Genoese poet Felice Romani, the man who had suggested *Il Pirata* as a subject and who was to collaborate with him on all but three of his operas. The two men enjoyed an exceptionally close artistic partnership. More than most operatic composers, Bellini was fastidious about his verse and regularly demanded rewrites. According to Romani, the showpiece aria, 'Casta diva', from Act I of *Norma*, went through no fewer than ten drafts before the composer professed himself satisfied.

The story for *Norma* is taken from the play of the same name by the French writer Alexandre Soumet. A tale of religious extremism, love, duty and betrayal, its principal appeal for Bellini lay in the complexity of the title character. This was to be sung by the composer's friend and muse, Giuditta Pasta, who had already had Donizetti's Anna Boleyn and Amina from *La Sonnambula* created for her. According to Stendhal, she had a 'burning energy [and] extraordinary dynamism that can electrify an entire theatre'. Initially, she baulked at 'Casta diva', claiming it to be beyond her capabilities. But Bellini managed to reassure her, and the aria has – partly thanks to Maria Callas – gone on to have a life of its own.

As a student at the Real Collegio di Musica in Naples, Bellini had received advice, as well as tuition, from the composer Giacomo Tritto:

If your compositions 'sing', your music will most certainly please...Therefore, if you train your heart to give you melody and then you set it forth as simply as possible, your success will be assured.

Bellini never forgot these words and became the leading exponent of the *bel canto* (literally, 'beautiful singing') school of opera. With the advent of Verdi and, more especially, Wagner, this style went markedly out of fashion, yet both

19th-century heavyweights are known to have admired their young predecessor. Bellini, Verdi wrote, created 'long, long, melodies such as no-one before', while the future author of *The Ring*, who seldom had a good word to say about his fellow composers, was effusive in his compliments of *Norma*.

Nowadays, it no longer seems contradictory to combine a love for the mysticism of Wagner with an affection for Bellini.

Recommended recording: Maria Callas, Franco Corelli, Christa Ludwig Nicola Zaccaria, Orchestra and Chorus of La Scala, Tullio Serafin, 1960

39

L'Elisir d'Amore (1832)

Gaetano Donizetti

The omens were not good. 'We have a German prima donna, a tenor who stammers, a *buffo* with the voice of a goat and a French bass who isn't worth much.' Such was Gaetano Donizetti's appraisal of the cast of his new opera *L'Elisir d'Amore* before the opening night on 12 May 1832. A few weeks later, Hector Berlioz's evening at the Teatro Canobbiana in Milan seemed to confirm the composer's fears:

> I found the theatre full of people talking in normal voices, with their backs to the stage. The singers, undeterred, gesticulated and yelled their lungs out in the strictest spirit of rivalry. At least I presumed they did, from their wide-open mouths; but the noise of the audience was such that no sound penetrated except the bass drum. People were gambling, eating supper in their boxes, etc, etc...

Berlioz concludes this account with an indictment of Italian 'philistinism', in which he accuses the denizens of one of the most musical nations in Europe of having no more respect for music than for the art of cooking: 'They want a score that, like a plate of macaroni, can be assimilated immediately without their having to think about it or even pay any attention to it.' In fact, *L'Elisir d'Amore* was hailed from its first performance and has remained one of the most popular and frequently performed comic operas.

Like his fellow *bel canto* composers, Rossini and Bellini, Donizetti was both prodigious and precocious. By the age of 30, he had 24 operas under his belt and, when he came to compose *L'Elisir d'Amore*, at the age of 34, he completed the task in a little over a month. With hearty choruses, patter-songs, dexterous duets and sparkling melodies, *L'Elisir d'Amore* bundles along for almost three hours without so much as a stumble in pace or quality. Although the 'elixir of love' turns out to be nothing more than cheap Chianti, as an elixir of happiness, Donizetti's masterpiece is hard to beat.

Recommended recording: Angela Gheorghiu, Roberto Alagna, Roberto Scaltriti, Simone Alaimo, Orchestre et Choeur de l'Opera National de Lyon, Evelino Pidò, Decca, 1996

40

Fantasy in C Major (1836)

Robert Schumann

No romantic musical partnership was more important or more fruitful than that of Robert and Clara Schumann. The daughter of a singer and a piano teacher, Clara Wieck trained as a pianist according to the precepts laid out in her father's treatise, *Clavier und Gesang* ('Piano and Song'). She made her debut at the Leipzig Gewandhaus, in October 1828, at the age of nine, the same year she met a young law student named Robert Schumann.

Nearly a decade older than Clara and also a talented pianist, Schumann had spent his adolescence juggling his twin passions for music and literature. In 1826, however, his father died and, conforming to the wishes of his mother and guardian, he began to study law at Leipzig University. Fortunately for posterity, Schumann spent considerably more time on music than he did memorising the 'ice-cold definitions' of the law. He began to take piano lessons from Friedrich Wieck in 1828 and, two years later, became a resident-pupil in his teacher's house. Wieck believed that Schumann had the potential to become the greatest pianist of his age but a hand injury caused the young man to focus on a career as a composer.

Meanwhile, Clara had gained a considerable reputation as a pianist, collecting paeans from Goethe, Paganini and Mendelssohn. She had also fallen in love with Schumann who, for his part, had grown increasingly attracted to the girl he now described as a 'pearl' for which you had to dive. In November 1835, he took the plunge, kissing Clara as she led him down the stairs of her father's house. The location was not exactly prudent. Wieck, who had been aware of Schumann's unofficial engagement to another of his pupils, was furious when he found out and banned the young lovers from seeing each other. When he discovered that the couple had met in secret, in February 1836, he forced Clara to sever all ties with Schumann, vowing to shoot his former pupil if he came near her again.

It was during their enforced separation, in the summer and autumn of 1836, that Schumann composed the first movement of what became his Fantasy in C for solo piano. Initially intended as a stand-alone movement, it constitutes a rhapsodic love letter to Clara, which Schumann considered 'perhaps the most passionate [piece] I have ever composed'. Later in the year, wishing to create a more substantial work that could be published to raise money for the campaign to erect a statue to Beethoven in his native Bonn, he added two more movements: a quasi-march and a slow movement 'played quietly throughout'.

Eventually published in May 1839, the Fantasy was formally dedicated to Franz Liszt but the lines from the poet

Friedrich Schlegel, with which Schumann prefaced the work, speak to the piece's true inspiration:

> Resounding through all the notes
> In the earth's colourful dream
> There sounds a faint long-drawn note
> For the one who listens in secret.

Recommended recording: Daniel Barenboim, Deutsche Grammophon, 1979

41

Scherzo No. 2 in B-flat Minor (1837)

Frédéric Chopin

For almost all of the composers in this book, the ultimate ambition was to express their artistry through large-scale orchestral works or opera. Frédéric Chopin stands alone among the great composers for focussing almost exclusively on the piano: an instrument whose full range and myriad possibilities he explored in over 60 mazurkas, 36 waltzes, 27 preludes, 21 nocturnes, 16 polonaises, 12 études, four ballades, four impromptus, four scherzi, three sonatas and two concertos.

In the Classical period, a *scherzo* (Italian for 'joke') was a light, dance-like movement, typically deployed in a symphony to act as a palate cleanser between the depth of the slow movement and the excitement of the finale. The Scherzo in Beethoven's Ninth Symphony moved decisively away from this tradition but it is Chopin's four Scherzi, written between 1831 and 1843, that bear no resemblance to the Classical model. No light relief here: these pieces are tempestuous and impassioned, requiring both virtuosity and subtlety on the part of the pianist. The Scherzo No. 2 in B-flat Minor is as romantic and rhapsodic as they come. An impetuous Presto, that juxtaposes soft lyricism with furious declamation, it was likened by Schumann to a poem by Byron, due to its 'overflowing tenderness, boldness, love and contempt'.

Recommended recording: Vladimir Ashkenazy, Decca, 1982

42

Piano Trio No. 1 in D Minor (1839)

Felix Mendelssohn

Mendelssohn, it has been said, played no great role in the development or teleology of classical music. Instructed in composition by the conservative Carl Friedrich Zelter, it was to the titans of the 18th century – Mozart, Haydn and Bach – that the composer looked for guidance and inspiration. Yet while Mendelssohn, unlike his contemporary Franz Liszt, was no musical revolutionary, it would be a serious mistake to underestimate his artistry.

Mendelssohn's Piano Trio No. 1 in D Minor contains elements of both Classicism and Romanticism. Elegant and formally structured, it is also melancholic, subjective and stormy. The emotional tone is set right from the start with the cello's distressed lament. Having produced a first draft of the work, Mendelssohn showed it to fellow composer Ferdinand Hiller. Hiller recommended revising the piano part, so as to give greater weight to the keyboard within the Trio. This is particularly evident in the final movement, *allegro assai appassionato* ('extremely lively and with passion'), which makes significant demands of the pianist, including sweeping arpeggios and chromatic octaves. It is one of many pieces by Mendelssohn without which the world would be decidedly poorer.

Recommended recording: Julia Fischer, Daniel Müller-Schott and Jonathan Gilad, Pentatone, 2006

43

Piano Quintet No. 1 in A Minor (1839)

Louise Farrenc

Louise Farrenc is not a household name. In her day, however, she was renowned as a pianist, teacher and composer. Born Jeanne-Louise Dumont into a distinguished line of court sculptors and female artists, she excelled at the piano from an early age and, by 15, was studying composition at the Paris Conservatoire. Her marriage to the flautist Aristide Farrenc in 1821 caused a hiatus in her studies, when the newly-weds embarked on a joint concert tour, but these resumed a few years later and, in general, her husband seems to have done everything he could to aid his wife's career – not least by publishing her early compositions.

Farrenc's first essays were solo piano works: rondos, variations on operatic arias and a set of études. Reviewing her *Variations on a Russian Air*, no less a critic than Schumann praised her 'auspicious talent and fine training'. Although he thought it possible that these 'small, neat, succinct studies' may have been written under the eye of her husband – now a successful music publisher – this in no way detracted from their charm and 'subtle aroma of romanticism'. Trying her hand at orchestral works, Farrenc produced two overtures in 1834, before going on to complete three symphonies during the 1840s. Writing in the *Gazette Musicale*, Berlioz described the second of these early overtures as 'well written and orchestrated with a talent rare among women' – a compliment that would not have been considered patronising at the time.

It is, however, for her chamber music that Farrenc most deserves to be remembered: for her Nonet, Trios and two Piano Quintets. Of these latter two works, composed in 1839 and 1840 respectively, it is hard to pick a favourite but I think, on balance, that the first, in A minor, with its Mendelssohnian feel, has the edge.

Farrenc's compositional output slowed towards the end of the 1850s, before ceasing entirely after the death of her daughter, also a celebrated pianist, at the age of 33. She did, however, continue to teach, having been appointed to the distinguished post of Professor of Piano at the Paris Conservatoire in 1842. Not only was Farrenc the only woman to hold a permanent post at the conservative Conservatoire during the course of the entire 19th century, she also managed, eventually, to achieve parity of pay with her male colleagues. Aware of the discrepancy, she had waited until after the triumphant premiere of her Nonet (scored for a combination of string quartet and wind quintet) in 1850 before tackling the Director of the Conservatoire, Daniel Auber. Her letter to him is a masterclass in reasonable firmness:

> I dare hope, M. Director, that you will agree to fix my fees at the same level as these gentlemen, because, setting aside

questions of self-interest, if I do not receive the same incentive they do, one might think that I have not invested all the zeal and diligence necessary to fulfil the task which has been entrusted to me.

Auber coughed up.

*Recommended recording: Quintetto Bottesini, Brilliant
Classics, 2014*

44

Nocturne No. 13 in C Minor (1841)

Frédéric Chopin

While the practitioners of the Enlightenment sought to dispel superstition and mystery with the light of rationalism, the Romantics were drawn to the night, where dreams are born and the imagination takes flight.

It was the Irish-born composer, John Field, who invented the nocturne – a lyrical piece suggestive of the night – but it was Chopin who brought immortality to the genre. His 21 nocturnes, written between 1827 and 1846, are for many people the apogee of his artistry and a case may be made for almost all of them. Yet, while the second, in E-flat, is the most well known, my favourite, which I fumble through on the piano, is No. 13 in C Minor.

With a slow melodic line, oscillating between the deep base and the upper register, the main theme is grief-filled and noble. After an extraordinary chorale, with octaves flying up and down the keyboard, the theme returns but *doppio movimento agitato* ('twice as fast and agitated'). The keys themselves seem to be singing in sweet distress as the music seethes and simmers before expiring with a sigh.

Recommended recording: Vladimir Ashkenazy, Decca, 1979

45

Polonaise in A-flat Major, 'Heroic' (1842)

Frédéric Chopin

1848, according to the great Whig historian G. M. Trevelyan, was 'the turning point at which modern history failed to turn'; the year in which Europe could and should have moved in a more liberal, democratic direction but, thanks to the failure of the revolutions which swept the continent, saw the reimposition of authoritarian, reactionary state control. For those involved at the time, however, it was a period of hope and excitement.

Amantine Lucile Aurore Dupin was better known by her pen name, George Sand. One of Europe's most popular novelists, she was also the lover of Chopin. An ardent republican, who became a member of the French Provisional Government, following the overthrow of King Louis Phillippe, Sand's reaction her amour's A-flat Polonaise, she was ecstatic: '*L'inspiration! La force! La vigueur!*' This was the spirit of the Revolution! This was the 'heroic symbol' that would inspire the insurrectionists.

In fact, Chopin – who did not like to confer descriptive titles on his works – had written the Polonaise six years earlier. There is, however, such dash and daring in this work, such individuality, verve and determination that the epithet, 'Heroic', conferred by Sand, seems more than justified.

Recommended recording: Maurizio Pollini, Deutsche Grammophon, 1976

46

Piano Concerto in A Minor
(1841–1845)
Robert Schumann

Prior to his marriage to Clara Wieck, Schumann had written almost exclusively for the voice and solo piano. It was Clara who encouraged him to undertake more ambitious projects. In May 1841, he completed a Fantasy in A Minor for Piano and Orchestra but, despite the performance given by his wife at the Leipzig Gewandhaus, the work failed to impress the publishers. Undeterred, Clara, who had already written her own piano concerto as a teenager, urged her husband to expand the piece. An Intermezzo and Allegro Vivace were duly added and, on 4 December 1845, Schumann's only piano concerto received its premiere with his wife as the soloist.

From an early age, Schumann was fascinated by the duality of the human psyche. 'It sometimes seems…as if my objective self wanted to separate itself completely from my subjective self,' he confided to his diary on his 21st birthday, 'or as if I stood between my appearance and my actual being, between form and shadow.' This dilemma was to become an increasingly tragic theme in the composer's life, as he alternated between bouts of depression and periods of mania (what would now, probably, be diagnosed as bipolar disorder). Even before he suffered his first mental collapse, in the autumn of 1833, he had identified two contrasting strands of his personality: the fiery improviser, whom he christened 'Florestan', and the introspective poet, 'Eusebius'.

Schumann's Piano Concerto is a conflict between these two characters. The piece opens with Florestan's dramatic descent down the keyboard, only to be halted by the dream-like Eusebius. Yet the concerto is also a love letter to Clara. Written in A minor, the same key as his wife's concerto, the opening Eusebius melody spells the Italian version of Clara's name in musical notes. After a dainty slow movement – which, as Schumann writes, is really no more than an Intermezzo between the two main movements – we move, seamlessly, into the A major Allegro Vivace. The doubts and struggles of the first movement have evaporated and love, it seems, has triumphed over adversity; the music, literally, leaping with joy.

Recommended recording: Murray Perahia, Bavarian Radio Symphony Orchestra, Colin Davis, Sony Classical, 1988

47

Tannhäuser (1843–1845 & 1861)

Richard Wagner

No composer has induced greater controversy than Richard Wagner. A visionary who created the most searing musical and dramatic experiences in all opera (arguably in all art), he was also a notorious anti-semite, later lauded by Hitler and the Nazis. His operas, several of which last for more than four hours, have provoked a plethora of quips and invective:

> 'Wagner has beautiful moments but awful quarter hours.'
> – Rossini

> 'Wagner's music is better than it sounds.' – Mark Twain

> 'The music of Wagner imposes mental tortures that only algebra has a right to inflict.' – Paul de Saint-Victor

> 'I love Wagner. But the music I prefer is that of a cat hung up by its tail outside a window and trying to stick to the panes of glass with its claws.' – Charles Baudelaire

Yet for the many millions who love his music, his operas constitute an almost religious experience. Staggering out of the opera house after a marathon session, with not one bar of light relief (*Die Meistersinger* excepted), our nerves a-jangle, our senses on fire, the Wagnerite can think of only one question: when can I hear it all again?

Wagner's operas fall into three distinct periods: his early operas – *Die Feen* ('The Fairies', 1834), *Das Liebesverbot* ('The Ban on Love', 1836) and *Rienzi* (1840), in which he tried to tailor his emerging genius to fit existing styles (*Rienzi* is really *Nabucco* with a German accent); his German Romantic operas – *The Flying Dutchman* (1841), *Tannhäuser* (1845) and *Lohengrin* (1848); and, finally, the mature music dramas, to which he applied some of the theories set out in his prose works (he abandoned many), as well as the philosophy of Schopenhauer – *Der Ring des Nibelungen* (1853–1874), *Tristan und Isolde* (1857–1859), *Die Meistersinger von Nürnberg* (1862–1867) and *Parsifal* (1877–1882). Of the middle period, there is no doubt in my mind that *Tannhäuser* is the greatest: the first of the composer's operas to which I became addicted.

Indeed, if I were to recommend one section of one piece to serve as an introduction to Wagner's genius, I would steer listeners to the overture to *Tannhäuser*, with its spine-tingling rendition of the Act III 'Pilgrim's Chorus'.

The opera, which deals with some of the themes that most obsessed Wagner – the dichotomy between sacred and profane love, the role of the artist within society and the quest for redemption – was composed between 1843 and 1845 but later revised for its presentation at the Paris Opera in 1861. Although the performance was an infamous debacle, which cemented the composer's loathing of the French capital, the true measure of it is captured in the prayer of the French composer Charles Gounod: 'God grant me such a failure!'

Recommended recording: René Kollo, Helga Dernesch, Christa Ludwig, Hans Sotin, Victor Braun, Werner Hollweg, Kurt Equiluz, Manfred Jungwirth, Norman Bailey, Vienna State Opera Chorus, Vienna Boys' Choir, Vienna Philharmonic, George Solti, Decca, 1970

48

Rigoletto (1850–1851)

Giuseppe Verdi

In a memorable scene in Willy Russell's *Educating Rita*, Frank, the clapped-out English don, tries to explain to Rita the difference between a tragedy and the merely tragic. A man killed by a falling tree is not a tragedy, he elucidates. 'It is for the poor sod under the tree,' she ripostes. No, he insists: it may be tragic but a tragedy requires an element of inevitability about the denouement. By this Aristotelian definition, *Rigoletto* may be the greatest tragedy in opera.

Taking their story from Victor Hugo's *Le roi s'amuse*, Verdi and his librettist, Francesco Maria Piave, deploy dramatic irony with unsparing brutality. Right from the opening scene, when Rigoletto, the hunchback court jester of the licentious Duke of Mantua, is cursed for encouraging his master's exploits, we know that we are in for trouble. When we learn that Rigoletto has a daughter, Gilda, whom he is hiding from the depraved court, our anxiety becomes acute. Condemned to remain one step ahead of the eponymous tragic hero, we watch in horror as Rigoletto is tricked into kidnapping his own daughter;

Gilda becomes the Duke's mistress; Rigoletto plots a flawed revenge; and Gilda commits an act of delusional self-sacrifice. A pinnacle of the grotesque comes as Rigoletto gloats over the sack 'containing' the body of the 'murdered Duke', only to hear the villain singing his vulgar tune, 'La donna è mobile' ('Woman is flighty'), into the night. Ripping open the bag, he reveals the truth we already know: *'Gilda! Mia Gilda!... È morta! Ah, la maledizione!'* (Gilda! My Gilda!...She is dead! Ah, the curse!).

Rigoletto belongs to that amazing three-year period, 1851–1853, which also saw the composition of *Il Trovatore* and *La Traviata* – a trinity which, alone, ensures Verdi's status as the supreme composer of Italian opera. In *Rigoletto*, Verdi took a new path. Seeking to create a more unified musical fabric, and with a dedication to the evolving tragedy, he wished to move beyond the traditional recitative, aria, chorus formulae and present, instead, 'an unbroken chain of duets'. This is not to say that he planned to eliminate the aria altogether. Aware just how catchy 'La donna è mobile' was, the composer refused to allow the tenor to see it before the dress rehearsal, lest it leak out of the opera house and start to be sung all over town. Yet it is the ensembles that form the backbone of the piece: the duets between Rigoletto and Gilda and, of course, the Act III quartet. Verdi admired the plays of Hugo and Schiller, and worshipped those of Shakespeare. Yet in this quartet, he demonstrates the advantage of opera over prose drama. While four people speaking at the same time – bearing their souls and revealing their motives – is just a noise, in opera it has the capacity to form a perfect harmony. Speaking to the baritone Felice Varesi, who sang the title character at the premiere of

Rigoletto on 11 March 1851, Verdi confessed his doubts that he would ever compose anything better than this quartet.

Recommended recording: Dietrich Fischer-Dieskau, Renata Scotto, Carlo Bergonzi, Ivo Vinco, Fiorenza Cossotto, Chorus and Orchestra of La Scala, Rafael Kubelik, Deutsche Grammophon, 1964

49

Cello Concerto in A Minor (1850)

Robert Schumann

Schumann composed his Cello Concerto – the first by a major composer since Haydn – shortly after his move from Dresden to Düsseldorf, where he succeeded Ferdinand Hiller as Municipal Director of Music in September 1850. His welcome could not have been more effusive and the years 1850–1853 were among his most productive, with roughly a third of his oeuvre composed during this period.

But his time in the west German city ended in calamity. After he fell out with the orchestra over his unorthodox (they would say incomprehensible) conducting style, a deterioration in his mental condition led to fears that he might unwittingly harm his wife. Early on the morning of 27 February 1854, he slipped out of the house and threw himself into the Rhine. An observant angler fished him out but it was the end of the composer's life. Transferred, at his own request, to a lunatic asylum near Bonn, he died on 29 July 1856.

Rich in tone and brooding in temperament, the opening orchestral *pizzicato* of the Schumann Cello Concerto sounds like raindrops on autumn leaves. Indeed, the whole piece has a distinctly autumnal feel: warm at times and intimate but with the ghost of a north wind.

Recommended recording: Heinrich Schiff, Berlin Philharmonic, Bernard Haitink, Philips, 1988

50

Piano Sonata in B Minor (1853)

Franz Liszt

Franz Liszt was the rock star of his day. Women fought over his gloves and handkerchiefs, kneeled before him in the street, fashioned his broken piano strings into bracelets, drained the dregs of his tea and, on at least one occasion, smoked the butt of his discarded cigar. That he was one of the most outstanding virtuoso pianists to have ever lived is beyond doubt. Yet as the poet and critic Heinrich Heine observed, there was more than an element of showmanship behind the disease he labelled 'Lisztmania'. Unlike previous pianists, who typically shared their recitals with singers and other musicians, Liszt's concerts were strictly solo performances ('*Le concert c'est moi,*' he once declared). Entering from the wings, the sharply chiselled Hungarian would sit at the piano – placed length wise so the audience could see his profile – slowly remove a pair of white gloves, push his long dark hair behind his ears and throw himself upon the instrument. The experience was anything but settling. 'He often rages all too madly upon the ivory keys,' complained Heine, 'and lets loose a deluge of heaven storming ideas, with here and there a few sweet flowers to shed fragrance upon the whole. One feels both blessedness and anxiety, but rather more anxiety.'

Although recalling one of the pianist's famous improvising sessions, this description could apply, with equal justice, to the B Minor Piano Sonata. Completed in 1853, this 30-minute, single-movement leviathan horrified some of its early listeners. 'This is nothing but a sheer racket,' exclaimed Clara Schumann. 'Not a single healthy idea, everything confused,' Johannes Brahms agreed, while the critic Eduard Hanslick declared that 'anyone who has heard it and finds it beautiful is beyond help'. Well, if this is the case, I am a lost cause. For me, as for most Liszt aficionados, the B Minor Sonata is the quintessence of the composer's genius. Fiendishly difficult, it is stormy, intricate, supremely romantic and vital.

Recommended recording: Krystian Zimerman, Deutsche Grammophon, 1990

51

Der Ring des Nibelungen (1853–1874)

Richard Wagner

Wagner's *Der Ring des Nibelungen* ('The Ring of the Nibelun-gen') constitutes the most ambitious project in western art. A cycle of four 'music dramas' – *Das Rheingold, Die Walküre, Siegfried and Götterdämmerung* – intended to be performed on successive nights, *The Ring* takes more than 16 hours to perform and took Wagner over a quarter of a century to cre-ate. True, he did not envisage the entire cycle from the very beginning. What started out as an idea for a single opera about the death of the legendary German hero, Siegfried, turned into plans for two operas, chronicling Siegfried's life and death, then three, to include Brünnhilde's story, and finally four, incorporating the original theft of the Rhinegold and the fashioning of the ring that gave the wearer the power to rule the world.

Yet it is not merely through its size that *The Ring* reveals its ambition. After finishing *Lohengrin*, in April 1848, Wagner set aside composing for six years while he undertook a com-plete reappraisal of the operatic form. In tracts such as *The*

Work of Art of the Future (1849), *Opera and Drama* (1851) and *A Message to my Friends* (1851), he fleshed out a new theory of opera, which he then applied, piecemeal, to parts of *The Ring*, before moving beyond his own theorising in *Tristan und Isolde*, *Die Meistersinger* and *Parsifal*.

Forests have been felled in the effort to elucidate Wagner's theories, as well as the influence of philosophers, such as Feuerbach and Schopenhauer, on his work. Suffice to say, Wagner had come to believe that opera – in theory the highest form of art – had degenerated to the level of mere social entertainment: a frivolous venture that allowed aristocrats and a burgeoning bourgeoisie to enjoy themselves and be seen enjoying themselves. What Wagner wished to create was art that would rival the plays of Ancient Greece: music dramas that would combine the poetic flights of Shakespeare with the musical expression of Beethoven. The subjects would be universal: myths that could deal with great philosophical questions and deep psychology. And the music would be the servant of the drama, not the other way around. Providing substance to this aim, Wagner developed the device with which his name is indelibly linked: the *leitmotif* – a musical phrase used to denote a particular character, object, place or idea that recurs throughout the drama. *The Ring* contains well over a hundred distinct *leitmotifs*, each subject to subtle changes and manipulation in order to reflect the developing mood and circumstances.

The plot of *The Ring* is wonderfully complex. To illustrate this with one genealogical point: Wotan, the King of the Gods, is the father or grandfather of nearly all the principal protagonists. He is the father of Siegmund and Sieglinde – the separated twins who, in *Die Walküre*, are reunited, fall in love and conceive Siegfried – and he is the father of the Valkyrie Brünnhilde who becomes the lover of his grandson, Siegfried. (Incest is only one of a number of grisly themes that appear in *The Ring*.)

Yet, viewed from afar, the meaning of *The Ring* may also be said to be destructively simple. Far from being a Marxist allegory (as Bernard Shaw argued) or any other kind of political manifesto, *The Ring* represents a devastating indictment of politics and an appeal to the inner self – most especially, to love. Time and again the gods, giants, dwarfs and men sacrifice love for power. (The only way the dwarf Alberich is able to steal the gold from the Rhinemaidens and forge the ring, in the first place, is by renouncing love.) Yet power does not merely corrupt, it destroys. One after the other, the characters of the cycle are consumed by the pursuit of the ring, until, in 'Götterdämmerung', the reign of the gods itself comes to an end and Valhalla, their shining palace in the sky, collapses into rubble. Only Brünnhilde goes the other way, forsaking her immortality for the love of a man. This does not save her but her immolation on Siegfried's funeral pyre – which also destroys the ring – sparks a new beginning for the world and offers us, the audience, a chance at redemption. 'Though I leave behind me a world without rulers,' declares Brünnhilde, in verses which Wagner wrote but, not wishing to be explicit, ultimately discarded, 'I now bequeath to that world my most sacred wisdom's hoard':

> Not wealth, not gold,
> Nor godly pomp;
> Not house, not garth,
> Nor lordly splendour,
> Not troubled treaties'
> Treacherous bonds,
> Not smooth-tongued custom's stern decree:
> Blessed in joy and sorrow
> Love alone can be.

This, of course, is only to blow the dust off the vast structure that is *The Ring*. It is, however, a mistake to be daunted by its sheer size and complexity. Although I am yet to see *The Ring* on stage (it is an unfortunate reality that to do so requires a week's holiday followed by an abstention from all other holidays, so great is the time and financial commitment) and cannot claim to have grasped more than a tenth of its meaning, I find myself overwhelmed just listening to it. They may be 'music dramas' but Wagner's genius manifests itself, first and foremost, through his music and this is something that can be appreciated by everyone. Start, then, by listening to *Die Walküre* and *Götterdämmerung* – the finest of the four parts – and embark on a journey of discovery that never ends.

Recommended recordings:

'Das Rheingold': Dietrich Fischer-Dieskau, Josephine Veasey, Simone Mangelsdorff, Martti Talvela, Karl Ridderbusch, Oralia Dominguez,

Robert Kerns, Zoltán Kelemen, Anna Reynolds, Edda Moser, Helen Donath, Berlin Philharmonic, Herbert von Karajan, Deutsche Grammophon, 1967

'Die Walküre': James King, Leonie Rysanek, Gerd Nienstedt, Birgit Nilsson, Theo Adam, Annelies Burmeister, Bayreuth Festival Orchestra, Karl Böhm, Decca, 1967

'Siegfried': Wolfgang Windgassen, Birgit Nilsson, Hans Hotter, Gerhard Stolze, Gustav Neidlinger, Kurt Böhme, Marga Höffgen, Joan Sutherland, Vienna Philharmonic, George Solti, Decca, 1962

'Götterdämmerung': Wolfgang Windgassen, Birgit Nilsson, Christa Ludwig, Dietrich Fischer-Dieskau, Claire Watson, Gustav Neidlinger, Gottlob Frick, Chorus of the Vienna State Opera, Vienna Philharmonic, George Solti, Decca, 1964

52

A Faust Symphony (1854/1857)

Franz Liszt

What would it feel like to make a pact with the Devil? Well, pretty terrifying, if Liszt's symphonic roller-coaster is anything to go by.

To say that the Romantics were fascinated by *Faust* – Goethe's dramatisation of the dissatisfied intellectual who sells his soul to Satan in exchange for one moment of pure transcendence – would be an understatement. Schubert set several songs to words from Goethe's tragedy, Schumann composed a secular oratorio on the play and Berlioz, in *Le damnation de Faust*, produced a hybrid of opera and cantata.

Initially, Liszt seems to have been wary about adding to this Faustiana. 'Anything having to do with Goethe is dangerous for me to handle,' he wrote to his lover, Princess Carolyne von Sayn-Wittgenstein. Yet, living in Weimar – the city of Goethe – made it hard to escape the subject, and a series of conversations with Mary Ann Evans, better known as George Eliot, and her consort, George Henry Lewes (who was writing a biography of Goethe) seems to have provided the final spur.

After a frenzy of composition, lasting a mere two months, Liszt completed his *Faust Symphony* in the autumn of 1854.

Instead of attempting to retell Goethe's story, Liszt decided to provide character sketches of the three principal protagonists. The first movement, which depicts Faust, ranges across a gamut of emotions from ennui to nostalgia, hedonism, passion and love. The second movement, which considers Faust's ill-fated lover, contains a dream-like duet for oboe and viola, suggestive of virginal innocence; while the final movement, dedicated to Mephistopheles, distorts the 'Faust' themes with diabolical ingenuity. Three years after completing the work, Liszt wrote a new ending, featuring Goethe's closing lines:

> Everything transitory
> Is only an allegory;
> What cannot be achieved,
> Here it will come to pass;
> What cannot be described
> Here it is accomplished;
> The Eternal Feminine
> Draws us aloft.

Still shocking, 150 years after it was composed, it is a piece that gets into the blood; like Faust, we have made a contract and are bound to continue listening for eternity.

Recommended recording: George Solti, Chicago Symphony Orchestra & Chorus, Decca, 1986

53

Tristan und Isolde (1857–1859)

Richard Wagner

'Since I have never in my life enjoyed the true happiness
of love, I intend to erect a further monument to this most
beautiful of dreams, a monument in which this love will be
properly sated from beginning to end.' So wrote Wagner to
Liszt, in December 1854, outlining his conception for an
opera based on the legend of *Tristan and Isolde*. In fact, as
anyone who has seen or even heard *Tristan und Isolde* knows,
love remains, notoriously, unsated. This is the whole point.
From the opening bar, which contains the celebrated 'Tristan
chord' – a harmonic sequence that fails to resolve and therefore leaves us in agonised suspense – the theme of the work is
the longing for love but the frustration of desire: a theme that
reaches its dramatic climax when the lovers' nocturnal tryst
is violently interrupted in Act II. Why, we may therefore ask,
did Wagner change his mind? Why, having originally decided
to write an opera about the satisfaction of romantic love, did
he end up writing an opera about the agony of desire; about
a love that can only be truly fulfilled in death? The answer lies

in two seminal events in the composer's life: his infatuation with the poet Mathilde Wesendonck and his discovery of the philosophy of Arthur Schopenhauer.

Otto Wesendonck was a prosperous silk merchant whose generosity saved Wagner from ruin. In the autumn of 1856, he invited the composer and his wife to come and live in a house adjacent to his own on the shores of Lake Zurich (a residency that began in the spring of the following year). Had he known the extent of Wagner's infatuation with his wife, the beautiful Mathilde, he might have thought twice. The passionate but almost certainly unconsummated affair between Wagner and Mathilde provided both the inspiration and prototype for *Tristan und Isolde*. 'Such was the unheard-of success brought about by the glorious love of the purest and most noble of women,' wrote the composer to his sister, 'and it was this love, to which we never gave expression, that was bound at last to reveal itself when I wrote the *Tristan* poem a year ago and gave it to her.'

The influence of Schopenhauer is more complicated. Wagner was swift to accept the philosopher's arguments, set out in *The World as Will and Representation*, that placed music on a higher plane than the other arts (this can be seen in *Tristan*, where the music itself becomes the protagonist, expressing states of emotion and being that words can only hint at). Yet while Wagner agreed with Schopenhauer that the sexual act offered the greatest insight into the self and its 'will to live', he drew the line at the philosopher's advocacy of sexual abstention – a deliberate denial of 'the will'. For Wagner (though he was often in two minds on the subject), sex was the ultimate expression of romantic love – a means, so he argued in

138

an unsent letter to the philosopher, of achieving transcendence. Yet, while *Tristan* is suffused with the yearnings of sexual desire, the hand of Schopenhauer is felt through the continued frustration of this desire, until the lovers realise that only through death will they achieve unity: 'Let us die and never part – united – nameless – endless – no more Tristan – no more Isolde.'

Considered a watershed in the history of music due to its use of dissonance and chromaticism, *Tristan und Isolde* is as intoxicating as the love potion the ill-fated pair drink at the start of Act I. A work which, Wagner believed, would 'drive people mad', it remains as 'dangerously fascinating' (Nietzsche) today as it must have seemed at its first performance on 10 June 1865.

Recommended recording: Plácido Domingo, Nina Stemme, Mihoko Fujimura, René Pape, Olaf Bär, Jared Holt, Ian Bostridge, Matthew Rose, Rolando Villazón, The Royal Opera Chorus, Orchestra of the Royal Opera House, Covent Garden, Antonio Pappano, 2005

54

Introduction et Rondo Capriccioso (1863)

Camille Saint-Säens

If Camille Saint-Säens's 'Introduction et Rondo Capriccioso' were an item of clothing it would, I feel, be categorised as a 'saucy little number', unsafe to be worn in front of great aunts or in the vicinity of horses.

Saint-Säens starts by lulling us into a false sense of security. The A minor Introduction is respectfully romantic, almost Mendelssohnian. There are flashes of brilliance but everything is kept within bounds. Then, with one crashing chord from the orchestra, the coat comes off and the violin begins strutting its stuff. Coquettish, conceited and capricious, the violin flaunts its virtuosity with dazzling insouciance. A wink here, a cheeky flourish there; it is as if the soloist is moving around some smoke-filled Parisian salon, seducing each table, before disappearing, in a blaze of pyrotechnics, behind a velvet curtain.

Composed in 1863 – with obvious debts to both Paganini and Spanish dance rhythms – the 'Introduction et Rondo

Capriccioso' was, originally, intended as the finale of Saint-Säens's first Violin Concerto. Its premiere, in April 1867, however, was so successful that the composer decided to keep it as a stand-alone piece. We can understand why.

Recommended recording: Pierre Amoyal, Vernon Handley, New Philharmonia Orchestra, RCA Red Seal, 1984

55

Petite Messe Solennelle (1863–1864)

Gioachino Rossini

We left Rossini getting fat and nursing a miscellany of ailments in Paris. For 30 years, he did little by way of composing. Then, at the age of 71, he bestirred himself and wrote what he described as 'the last sin of my old age'. This was the *Petite Messe Solennelle* ('Little Solemn Mass').

The *Petite Messe* is one of the most unusual pieces on this list. Originally scored for two pianos and harmonium, with four soloists and a choir of no more than eight singers, its syncopated, nervous beginning sounds almost like jazz. Later we hear echoes of Palestrina, nods to Mozart and reminiscences of the composer's own *bel canto* days, while occasionally wondering if we are not on some hallucinogenic trip in a southern blues bar. 'Is this sacred music that I have written or is it wicked music?' Rossini asks 'God' in the preface to the score. 'I was bred for *opera buffa* as you know all too well. A little skill, a little heart, that is all. Be blessed, then, and admit me to Paradise.' This tongue-in-cheek dedication, it has been suggested, may be evidence of a lack of faith on the part of the composer, whose 'Little Solemn Mass', it has to be said, is neither little, nor particularly solemn. Yet for all its irony and playfulness, the *Petite Messe* has moments of true spiritualism, (the soprano-contralto duet in the 'Qui tollis peccata mundi), while the notion that Rossini was a composer of only 'little skill' is demolished in this most idiosyncratic of musical masterpieces as surely as in any of his operas.

Recommended recording: Krassimira Stoyanova, Birgit Remmert, Steve Davislim, Hanno Müller-Brachmann, Ryoko Morooka, Philip Mayers, Philip Moll, RIAS-Kammerchor, Marcus Creed, Harmonia Mundi, 2000

56

Roméo et Juliette (1865–1867)

Charles Gounod

Probably the most famous, secular story in the western world, Shakespeare's tragic love tale has inspired at least 24 operas, a *symphonie dramatique* by Berlioz, an overture by Tchaikovsky, a ballet by Prokofiev and a musical by Leonard Bernstein.

Roméo and Juliette is, of course, set in medieval Verona. Charles Gounod's adaptation is broadly faithful to the play but, make no mistake, this is French opera in all its 19th-century splendour. Opening with a crashing overture – the trombones depicting the 'ancient grudge' broken to 'new mutiny' between the Capulets and the Montagues – we are then treated to a series of sumptuous choruses and several show-stopping arias, the most famous of which, Juliet's 'Je veux vivre dans ce rêve qui m'enivre' ('I want to live in this dream that intoxicates me'), was surely inspired by Violetta's 'Sempre libera' from *La Traviata*.

Yet it is in the intimate scenes that Gounod excels and propels *Romeo and Juliet* into the Pantheon of Romantic opera. Over the course of four duets, he traces the development of the 'star-crossed' protagonists, from shy strangers to impassioned lovers, to, ultimately, tragic heroes. Voluptuous yet tender, dramatic yet intimate, it is music that conveys the love which 'looks on tempests and is never shaken'.

Recommended recording: Franco Corelli, Mirella Freni, Xavier Depraz, Henri Gui, Orchestre et Choeur du Théâtre National de l'Opéra de Paris, Alain Lombard, 1968

57

Don Carlos (1867–1886)

Giuseppe Verdi

You are a young man, walking in a forest, when you come across a beautiful woman. She is cold. You light a fire to keep her warm. She turns out to be the daughter of the French King. This is fortunate since you are the son of the Spanish King, betrothed to said Princess as part of a peace treaty between the two countries. You fall in love, enjoy approximately four minutes of happiness (one aria) and then a messenger arrives to say that the terms of the treaty have been changed and that the Princess is now to marry the King, not the Infante. You are now in love with your stepmother. Awkward.

Based on the play by Schiller, *Don Carlos* is both the longest and the grandest of Verdi's operas. Commissioned for the Paris Opera in 1867, it conforms to the French concept of 'grand opera', with palaces and cathedrals, large choruses, elaborate scenery and even ballet. The finale of Act III is particularly spectacular. In front of the cathedral of Our Lady of Atocha, the people and the Spanish Court gather for the public burning of heretics, condemned by the Inquisition.

Bells peal, violin bows ricochet and kettledrums roll, as the people celebrate the imminent demise of the unbelievers. Then, the music changes as a simple, sinister pulse marks the entry of the monks, leading the condemned to the stakes. After a scene-stopping confrontation between the Infante and his father, Carlos is arrested and the woodpiles are ignited. The curtain falls as the monks extol the 'Day of Wrath' and the people celebrate the 'Glory of God'. This is 16th-century Spain in all its power and darkness.

Recommended recording: Plácido Domingo, Katia Ricciarelli, Lucia Valentini Terrani, Leo Nucci, Ruggero Raimondi, Nicolai Ghiaurov, Chorus and Orchestra of La Scala, Claudio Abbado, Deutsche Grammophon, 1984

58

Tales from the Vienna Woods (1868)

Johann Strauss II

Johann Strauss II composed over 500 waltzes, polkas, quadrilles and other dances. Known as the 'Waltz King' (a title once held by his father, Johann Strauss I, author of the famous *Radetzky March*), he was once considered to be one of the three most famous people in Europe, alongside Queen Victoria and Otto von Bismarck. Admired by such musical heavyweights as Brahms, Wagner and Richard Strauss (no relation), he received mock commiserations from Giuseppe Verdi on the occasion of celebrations to mark the 50th anniversary of his first public concert:

> I am sorry for Signor Strauss. His enthusiastic admirers will devour him. I admire him as a highly gifted colleague. The best I can wish him is good health. He will need it. To be called Strauss and have jubilee in Vienna – may God help him!

Listened to superficially, Strauss's music can seem...well, superficial. Conjuring images of champagne flutes and gilded ballrooms, it is easily dismissed as decadent and frothy. But dig beneath the surface and you discover a countervailing melancholy that elevates his music far above that of other popular dance composers (Berlioz, another admirer, said that Strauss's melodies always made him feel deeply sad). This duality is especially evident in the 1868 waltz, 'Tales from the Vienna Woods'. After a long introduction, a solo violin establishes the main theme, which is both happy and sad, bright and nostalgic, all at the same time.

Recommended recording: Vienna Philharmonic, Willi Boskovsky, Decca, 1962

59

Siegfried Idyll (1870)

Richard Wagner

Notoriously, Wagner was not always the most uxorious of men. Having married the actress Christine Wilhelmine ('Minna') Planer in 1836, he went on to have several infatuations and affairs, including with the poet Mathilde Wesendonck. Later, he fathered three children with Cosima von Bülow, daughter of Liszt and wife of his most enthusiastic interpreter, the conductor Hans von Bülow, before marrying her in August 1870. (Von Bülow's response to Cosima's request for a divorce is unbearably pathetic:

> Since you left me I have been deprived of my whole support in dealing with life and its struggles...[But] you have preferred to consecrate the treasures of your mind and heart to a higher being: far from censuring you for this step, I approve it.)

Even for the formidable Cosima, life with Wagner was not always easy (in 1876, the composer began an affair with the French poet and novelist, Judith Gautier). Yet to his second wife, Wagner made the supreme romantic gesture. The year was 1870 and the newly married couple were staying at their villa at Tribschen, on the edge of Lake Lucerne. On Christmas morning, Cosima woke to the sound of music. At first, she thought she was dreaming. But then she roused herself and realised that the music was emanating from a small ensemble. When the performance was over, Wagner entered her bedroom and presented her with a score entitled 'Tribschen Idyll with Fidi's birdsong and the orange sunrise, as symphonic birthday greeting'. Cosima, who had turned 33 the day before, wrote in her diary, 'I was in tears, but so, too, was the whole household. Richard had set up his orchestra on the stairs and thus consecrated our Tribschen forever!'

'Fidi' was the couple's nickname for their newborn son, Siegfried. Later, Wagner would incorporate the theme from what became known as the 'Siegfried Idyll' into the third part of his *Ring* cycle of the same name. The piece, however, is indisputably Cosima's: a love letter that feels like a warm breeze on Alpine pastures.

Recommended recording: Swedish Chamber Orchestra, Thomas Dausgaard, BIS, 2012

60

Pictures at an Exhibition (1874)

Modest Mussorgsky

For those who regard Tchaikovsky as Russia's greatest composer, it may come as a surprise to learn that he was not a
member of that 'club' of leading late-19th-century Russian
composers, known as 'The Five' or, even more grandly, 'The
Mighty Handful', consisting of Mily Balakirev, César Cui,
Modest Mussorgsky, Nikolai Rimsky-Korsakov and Alexander
Borodin. These St Petersburg-based composers – all of whom
were self-trained amateurs – strove to create an 'authentically
Russian' sound, freed from the constraints of the conservatoire. In this they were considered, and considered themselves,
to be different to the more 'western-oriented' Tchaikovsky
(though it is hard to think of anything more Russian than
the Fourth Symphony, let alone the *Marche Slave*): a Russian
nationalist school of composers no less.

Viktor Hartmann was a painter and architect who had
begun his career as a book illustrator. A close friend of Mussorgsky's, he shared the composer's enthusiasm for new, intrin-
sically Russian art and gave him two of his paintings. When

Hartmann died in 1873, the critic Vladimir Stasov arranged a posthumous exhibition of his works and it was from this that Mussorgsky derived the inspiration for his most famous composition.

Pictures at an Exhibition is a classic example of 'programme music': music, which depicts or evokes a particular event, narrative, idea or feeling, external to the music itself. (Other notable examples include Vivaldi's *Four Seasons*, Beethoven's 'Pastoral' Symphony, Berlioz's *Symphonie fantastique*, Saint-Saëns' *Carnival of the Animals* and all ten of Richard Strauss's tone poems). In this case, the programme is the exhibition. The confidant 'Promenade' theme, sees the composer stride purposefully through the gallery Suddenly, he stops. The first canvas, evoked by a scuttling motif and eerie chromaticism, shows a gnome running about with 'crooked legs'. It is an unsettling image but, soon, the composer is off again on his travels, this time towards a melancholy setting of an old castle. Other pictures reveal children quarrelling in the Tuileries gardens (Hartmann had spent the majority of his career abroad), a lumbering cart driven by oxen, the murky world of the Parisian catacombs and, finally, the Bogatyr Gates in Kiev. Extraordinarily modern – the evocation of the 'Market at Limoges' prefigures Prokofiev's *Romeo and Juliet* (1940), while other sections sound uncannily like Bernard Herrmann's score for Alfred Hitchcock's *North by Northwest* – Mussorgsky's piano suites have been the subject of numerous orchestrations, the most successful of which was undertaken by Maurice Ravel in 1922.

Recommended recording: Gustavo Dudamel, Vienna Philharmonic, Deutsche Grammophon, 2016

61

Messa da Requiem (1874)

Giuseppe Verdi

'Now it is finished! And with him dies the purest, holiest, and highest of our glories.' Such were Giuseppe Verdi's feelings following the death of the poet and writer Alessandro Manzoni, whose 1827 novel *I Promessi Sposi* ('The Betrothed') the composer considered 'not only the greatest book of our time but one of the greatest books that the human mind has produced'. Ten days later, he wrote to his publisher, Ricordi, and announced his intention of honouring Manzoni by composing a great Requiem Mass, to be performed on the first anniversary of the writer's death.

It was not the first time that Verdi had embarked on such a project. Six years earlier, when Rossini died, he had proposed a collaboration between the leading Italian composers of the day to produce a musical monument to the late composer.

The *Messa per Rossini* was duly written but, thanks to a series of quarrels over the proposed performance, was never heard. Now, Verdi had the chance to resurrect his contribution – the final part of the Mass, the Libera me – in his own, solely authored, Requiem.

There is no denying the dramatic, even theatrical, quality of Verdi's Requiem. The renowned 19th-century conductor Hans von Bülow notoriously described the work as 'opera in ecclesiastical robes'. Yet while there is some truth in the accusation (some would say, 'compliment'), the Requiem is also different from the composer's stage works: a profoundly spiritual, if not traditionally religious, piece, Verdi treats the text with respect, even while painting it in the most vivid colours. What it is not is academic. Verdi's music is visceral. From the hushed intonations at the start of the Requiem, to the fire and brimstone of the Dies irae, Verdi shows his determination to make us feel each section of the Mass as it unfolds. Thus, we experience grief (the *sotto voce* Requiem), terror before divine judgement (the Dies irae, with its trumpets and off-beat bass drum), joy (the Sanctus fugue), prayer (Agnus Dei) and, finally, desperation (the soprano pleading, in the Libera me, for salvation). Whether 'the greatest opera Verdi never wrote', or a major sacred work, the *Messa da Requiem* is among the most powerful pieces of music bequeathed to humanity.

Recommended recording: Anja Harteros, Sonia Ganassi, Rolando Villazón, René Pape, Orchestra e Coro dell'Accademia Nazionale di Santa Cecilia, Antonio Pappano, EMI, 2009

Carmen (1875)

Georges Bizet

Although technically an *opéra comique*, there is nothing funny about *Carmen*. A tale of promiscuity, jealousy and murder, it scandalised Parisian audiences when it was first performed and provoked the resignation of one of the directors of the Théâtre Opéra Comique. 'I sense defeat,' wailed the 36-year-old Georges Bizet, who had already endured several operatic failures, after the opening night: 'I foresee a definite and hopeless flop.' In fact, *Carmen* was acclaimed when it was premiered at the Vienna State Opera in October 1875 (Brahms saw it no fewer than 20 times) and went on to become one of the most popular and performed works in operatic history. It was, however, too late for Bizet. Disappointed and disillusioned by the dwindling audiences and attacks in the press, the composer, already battling quinsy and rheumatism, suffered a double heart attack and died on 3 June 1875, three months after unveiling *Carmen* to the world.

As well as the immorality of the libretto (a curious prudery for the inhabitants of a city which Zola described as 'the bawdy house of Europe'), *Carmen* was criticised for being Wagnerian. What this actually meant was that Bizet had refused to serve up the usual soufflé of trite frivolity on which the Parisian bourgeoisie liked to dine. (Fourteen years earlier, Wagner had been forced to withdraw the newly revised *Tannhäuser* from the Paris Opera, after the first three performances were interrupted by hecklers.) Indeed, aside from the use of *leitmotifs* for the leading characters, it is hard to think of an opera more removed from the mist and maelstrom of *The Ring* and *Tristan und Isolde* than *Carmen*: a piece which magnificently captures the vitality and sensuousness of post-Napoleonic Spain.

After the rumbustious overture, which reveals Bizet's talent as an orchestrator ('If you want to learn how to orchestrate, do not study Wagner's scores, study the score of *Carmen*,' declared Richard Strauss), the opening scenes establish the gentle rhythms of life in 1820s Seville – rhythms (and harmonies) that Carmen, the gypsy and ultimate femme fatale, will soon disrupt. Don José's Act I duet with the innocent Micaëla is fabulously lyrical, while Carmen's entrance aria, the famous 'Habanera', is surely the greatest expressions of raw sex appeal in 'classical' music. Other highlights include the accelerating gypsy dance that evokes the seedy underworld of Pastia's Inn at the start of Act II and Escamillo's swaggering entrance aria, the purposefully popular 'Toreador song'. Act III becomes increasingly dark as Don José's jealousy reaches fever pitch and cards predict Carmen's untimely death.

Although Act IV opens with the festivity of the overture and the 'Toreador' theme – the musical setting for the coming bull fight – it can only end one way and Bizet leaves us with one of the most powerful and dramatic confrontation scenes in opera. Thirteen years after the first performance, Friedrich Nietzsche, who had turned violently against his earlier advocacy of Wagner, described *Carmen* as the perfect representation of human love in all its primeval passion:

> Love as fate, fatality, cynical, innocent cruel love – and thus true to *nature*...Love in its ways is the war of the sexes, its basis their *mortal hatred*. I do not know any other instance where tragic humour, which constitutes the essence of love, is expressed more absolutely, in a more shattering phrase, than in Don José's last words:

> > *C'est moi qui l'ai tuée, ma Carmen,*
> > *Ma Carmen adorée!*
> > ['I killed her. Ah, my beloved Carmen!']

Recommended recording: Teresa Berganza, Plácido Domingo, Ileana Cotrubas, Sherrill Milnes, The Ambrosian Singers, London Symphony Orchestra, Claudio Abbado, Deutsche Grammophon, 1977

63

Slavonic Dances (1878 & 1886)

Antonín Dvořák

Antonín Dvořák did not enjoy the heady sensations of early success. The son of a butcher and innkeeper, from rural Bohemia, his early life was one of impoverishment and obscurity. Having studied the organ in Prague, he earned his crust playing the viola in a dance band, before the ensemble was subsumed into the orchestra for the Bohemian Provisional Theatre. By 1877, despite a number of his compositions having been performed, the 36-year-old composer was relying on a meagre income as a piano tutor and grants from the Austro-Hungarian state in order to survive. 1877, however, was the year Dvořák's fortunes changed.

Among the jurists for the state stipend was the 44-year-old Johannes Brahms. Brahms recognised Dvořák's talents and wrote to his publisher, Fritz Simrock, urging him to print his 'Moravian Motets'. Not only did Simrock acquiesce, he asked Dvořák to write something else – something dance-like. The result was his *Slavonic Dances*.

Dvořák took as his model Brahms's hugely popular

Hungarian Dances. Yet, while Brahms employed existing Hungarian folk tunes as the basis for the majority of his set, Dvořák's dances are entirely original compositions. Simrock published them in 1878 – first as piano duets then as orchestral pieces – and Dvořák suddenly found himself famous. There was a 'positive assault on the sheet music shops', wrote Berlin's leading music critic and, within months, the dances had been performed in Dresden, Hamburg, Berlin, London, Nice and New York. In 1886, at Simrock's request, Dvořák wrote a second, no less popular, set.

Exuberant, rustic, nostalgic and sensual, Dvořák's *Slavonic Dances* capture the rural Bohemia of his childhood.

Recommended recording: Jiří Bělohlávek, Czech Philharmonic Orchestra, Decca, 2014

64

Violin Concerto in D Major (1878)

Johannes Brahms

Music, by its very nature, is a collaborative art. Unless writing for a solo instrument, with their own performance principally in mind (like Chopin, Paganini or Liszt), composers must rely on a host of other musicians to bring their vision to life. Nor is it simply a question of performance: from poets and librettists to individual singers and soloists, the range of people who can inspire and shape a piece of music is prodigious.

The friendship between Johannes Brahms and the Hungarian violinist and composer Joseph Joachim began in the summer of 1853, when Brahms stayed in Joachim's rooms at the University of Göttingen. Two years older than Brahms and already established as a concert violinist, Joachim had been a protégé of Mendelssohn's, and would go on to earn the epithet 'Der Geigerkönig' ('The Violin King'). Brahms had been deeply impressed by a performance he had heard Joachim give of Beethoven's Violin Concerto, while Joachim, for his part, claimed that he had never been 'more completely overwhelmed' as when he heard the young Brahms's compositions.

Over the next decade, the two men would carouse and play together, with Joachim also providing the spur for Brahms's other great musical association: his lifelong friendship with Robert and Clara Schumann.

Brahms began work on his Violin Concerto shortly after completing his spring-like Second Symphony, in the summer of 1878. Written for and dedicated to Joachim, the composer relied on the violinist for technical advice and even allowed him to write his own cadenza. The piece was premiered in Leipzig on New Year's Day 1879. Although it drew a sceptical response from the critics – many of whom considered the violin part too difficult – its reception at its Viennese premiere, a few months later, was rapturous.

As well as one of the most lyrical slow movements – an *adagio* reminiscent of a lullaby – the piece contains the most optimistic finale: a joy-filled *allegro*, with all the vitality and flare of a gypsy dance.

Recommended recording: Janine Jansen, Orchestra dell'Accademia Nazionale di Santa Cecilia, Antonio Pappano, Decca, 2015

65

Eugene Onegin (1879)

Pyotr Ilyich Tchaikovsky

We know Tchaikovsky principally for his orchestral music: for his ballets, concertos and symphonies. Yet his ten complete operas and numerous false starts, spread over the course of his career, attest to his desire to be regarded as a serious opera composer. Unfortunately, many of his efforts were ill-conceived and, today, only *Eugene Onegin* and *The Queen of Spades* are regularly performed. Of these two, there is little doubt that the former is Tchaikovsky's operatic masterpiece.

It was the singer Elizaveta Lavrovskaya who suggested that Tchaikovsky create an opera from Pushkin's classic verse-novel. Initially, the composer was sceptical but enthusiasm soon overcame doubt and he began work on Tatyana's famous 'Letter' aria in the summer of 1877, completing the orchestration of the opera eight months later. Not that music was the only thing on his mind. In June 1877, despite or because of his homosexuality, Tchaikovsky proposed to a young woman named Antonina Miliukova, and this period, therefore, also contained his disastrous 11-week marriage, a complete nervous breakdown and, possibly, a suicide attempt. The wonderfully vivid evocations of love, rejection and emotional crisis in *Eugene Onegin* were, it seems, not drawn from Pushkin alone.

Eugene Onegin is a self-consciously domestic opera. Eschewing the grandeur of Verdi and the mythology of Wagner, Tchaikovsky set out to compose an opera which dealt with 'everyday, down to earth human experiences'. Time and again, he emphasised that his was not a subject containing 'tsars and tsarinas, popular rebellion, battles and marches'. Theatrical effects were to be kept to a minimum and the work, he stipulated, should be performed by talented amateurs, rather than ageing professionals. The result – first appearing under the modest subtitle 'Lyrical Scenes in Three Acts' – is among the most convincing, as well as the most beautiful, studies of human psychology in music.

Recommended recording: Dmitri Hvorostovsky, Nuccia Focile, Neil Shicoff, Orchestre de Paris, St Petersburg Chamber Choir, Semyon Bychkov, Philips, 1992

66

Cello Sonata in A Minor (1882–1883)

Edvard Grieg

Edvard Grieg is celebrated as Norway's pre-eminent composer: the man whose lyrical and nostalgic melodies harked back to a simpler, more rural past while, at the same time, helping to define a sense of contemporary Norwegian national identity. His best-known works, his Piano Concerto and Peer Gynt Suites have suffered through overfamiliarity (hardly Grieg's fault!) but there are dozens of lesser-known works – miniatures for the piano and over a hundred songs – which are well worth exploring.

Grieg wrote his one and only Cello Sonata between the summer of 1882 and the spring of the following year. It was not a happy time in the composer's life. Holed up in Hardanger, in western Norway, he was ill and felt creatively moribund. An attempt to write a second piano concerto had failed and his marriage to the singer Nina Hagerup was under strain. His inner turmoil found its way into the Cello Sonata, a piece that recalls and even quotes from his breakthrough success: his A Minor Piano Concerto.

The first movement – also in A minor – is tempestuous and impassioned: the piano and cello attacking the score and sparring off each other. The second movement is marked *andante molto tranquillo*, yet the agitation remains, enhanced by a sense of foreboding, intermingled with tragedy. Only in the final movement do the squalls subside, allowing the odd shaft of light to penetrate the clouds above the North Sea.

Recommended recording: Truls Mørk, Jean-Yves Thibaudet, Erato, 1988

67

Symphony No.4 in
E Minor (1884–1885)

Johannes Brahms

Brahms approached the symphony with trepidation. Beethoven cast a long shadow and the younger composer was acutely aware that anything he produced would be compared to the Master's nine hallowed symphonies. Thus, while he began sketches for a symphony in 1854, it was not until 1876 that he finally completed his first essay in the genre. Vindicating both his apprehension and his effort, the conductor, Hans von Bülow, dubbed it 'Beethoven's Tenth'. Having crossed the Rubicon, Brahms produced the sunny Second Symphony the following year and the mountainous Third in 1883.

Brahms decided to try out his Fourth Symphony, written between 1884 and 1885, on two pianos, before a small audience of musical friends. They were *not* enthusiastic. At the end of the first movement, composer's critical standard-bearer, Eduard Hanslick, memorably remarked that he felt as if he had just been 'beaten up by two terribly intelligent people'. Fortunately, the composer was not deterred, and, following the warm reception the symphony received at its premiere, on 25 October 1885, it began its history as a cornerstone of the symphonic repertoire.

The first movement of the Fourth Symphony has an elegiac, autumnal feel; its lilting theme at once doleful and nostalgic. The slow movement, by contrast, is filled with warm colours, while the Scherzo is positively ebullient. But the fourth movement...the fourth movement is deeply tragic. For the finale, Brahms resurrected the Baroque *passacaglia* – a series of variations over a short, repeated theme – and even took a tune from Bach's cantata *Nach dir, Herr, verlanget mich* ('For Thee, O Lord, I long') as his subject. Over 30 variations, we are sucked further and further down the vortex, before being confronted with a cataclysmic coda. It is almost as if Brahms, having struggled for so long with the symphonic inheritance of Beethoven, only to overcome it, was determined to destroy the entire edifice, leaving only memories amid the rubble.

Recommended recording: Carlos Kleiber, Vienna Philharmonic, Deutsche Grammophon, 1980

68

Otello (1884–1885)

Giuseppe Verdi

Otello is, arguably, the perfect opera. Pacey and compact, Verdi does not waste a note as he leads us through this agonising tale of love, jealousy and murder.

Like many 19th-century artists, Verdi venerated Shakespeare. 'To copy the truth can be a good thing, but to *invent the truth* is better…ask Papa about it,' he wrote to a friend in 1876. 'Papa' was not the composer's father – a recently deceased innkeeper and farmer from the Po Valley – but Shakespeare. In 1847, he had unveiled his take on *Macbeth* and, at various times, toyed with *Romeo and Juliet*, *Hamlet* and *The Tempest* as possible subjects. He longed to turn *King Lear* into an opera but, despite commissioning several librettos, was ultimately overwhelmed by the sheer magnitude of the challenge. *Otello*, with its three principal characters, was better suited to opera. The poet and polymath Arrigo Boito wrote the libretto (cutting the whole of Shakespeare's first act) and, after much coaxing, Verdi got down to serious work in the winter of 1884.

Otello is searing in its drama and passion. Opening with a thunderous chord that makes you jump out of your seat, you are immediately caught up in the storm which threatens to drown the Venetian fleet and foreshadows the coming tragedy. Verdi had not written a complete opera since *Aida* in 1871 and his style had developed over the 13-year hiatus. Although he had dabbled in dark colours in *Don Carlos*, his palette for *Otello* was yet more sinister and varied, with fewer set-piece arias and a greater interest in musical characterisation. Thus, while Verdi was content for Iago, as the embodiment of evil, to simply declaim his villainy (except when deceiving Otello, when he sings more sweetly), Desdemona, whom the composer considered an 'angel', sings with the innocent lyricism of an earlier age. As for the eponymous hero (or anti-hero), Verdi recognised how Otello had both to 'sing and shout' as he moves from warrior, to lover, to debased husband and, finally, murderer.

Recommended recording: Plácido Domingo, Cheryl Studer, Sergei Leiferkus, Orchestre et Choeurs de l'Opéra Bastille, Myung-Whun Chung, Deutsche Grammophon, 1993

69

Symphony No. 7 in
D Minor (1884–1885)

Antonín Dvořák

Dvořák was a trainspotter before it was fashionable. A steam obsessive, he haunted railway stations, noting arrival and departure times, befriended railway workers and declared, in complete seriousness, that he would gladly give up his symphonies in exchange for having invented the locomotive. One day in 1884, he was, as usual, at Prague's Franz Josef I terminus, where he watched as a train from Pest disgorged a crowd of his fellow countrymen, come to the Bohemian capital to attend a concert in aid of the Czech struggle for national identity. The patriotic Dvořák was stirred, and it was in this moment, he later claimed, that the portentous melody of the opening movement of his Seventh Symphony flashed across his mind.

The Seventh is the most dramatic and crepuscular of Dvořák's symphonies. While the first movement contains all the turmoil and idealism associated with nationalist struggle, the second is more personal. Dvořák provides the footnote

'From the sad years', and indeed, it seems that this exquisite slow movement was a reflection of the grief the composer felt following the recent deaths, not only of his mother but also of his eldest child. Chinks of light appear in the third movement – a Scherzo with echoes of the *Slavonic Dances* – before we plunge back into the mêlée with an impassioned Allegro: an expression, the composer later wrote, of the indomitable spirit of the Czech nation in the face of political oppression.

Although less well known and less frequently performed than his Ninth ('From the New World'), there is no doubt in my mind that this is the composer's masterpiece.

Recommended recording: Colin Davis, Royal Concertgebouw Orchestra, Philips, 1975

70

Symphony No. 7 in E Major (1883–1885)

Anton Bruckner

In the film version of Peter Shaffer's *Amadeus*, the soprano Caterina Cavalieri asks Salieri what Mozart looks like.

'You may be disappointed,' the Director of Italian Opera replies.

'Why?' she enquires.

'Because looks and talent do not always go together.'

Unlike much of Shaffer's play, this observation may have had a basis in fact. Compared to Bruckner, however, Mozart was an Adonis.

With a hooked nose, cannonball head, close-cropped hair and no neck to speak of, Anton Bruckner looked more like an Austrian pugilist than a composer. He was, however, one of the greatest symphonists of the 19th century.

Bruckner had more than his fair share of neuroses. Ambivalent about his talent (which his contemporaries frequently failed to recognise), he also suffered from 'number mania' – what today would probably be diagnosed as obsessive-compulsive disorder. Observed trying to count the leaves on a tree, he was no less fastidious in noting the number of spots on a window, pearls on a necklace or bars in his scores. For the first 20 years of his musical life, he composed almost exclusively for the church, before, in the 1860s, turning his attention to symphonies. Despite the vituperation of the critics ('We recoil in horror before this rotting odour which rushes into our nostrils from the disharmonies of this putrefactive counterpoint') and the hostility of the concert-going Viennese (most of the audience walked out during the premiere of his Third Symphony), Bruckner persisted and, by 1881, had completed nine (though two were subsequently withdrawn).

The Seventh is the most ethereal of Bruckner's symphonies. Opening with a *pianissimo* string *tremolo* – the subtlest of transitions from silence to sound, which Bruckner claimed came to him in a dream – the first movement floats on gentle contours towards a heart-bursting climax. The second movement levitates even further above the toil and tribulations of the terrestrial world. Composed as the 69-year-old Wagner was dying, it is a loving tribute to the man Bruckner referred to as the 'Meister aller Meister'. With the start of the Scherzo, a note of menace enters the piece for the first time but soon gives way to a lively dance. The finale, which begins in the same hushed manner as the first movement, builds to a brass-filled coda worthy of this epic.

Recommended recording: Royal Concertgebouw Orchestra, Bernard Haitink, Decca, 1966

71

Cello Sonata No. 2 in F Major (1886)

Johannes Brahms

In *Brideshead Revisited*, Charles Ryder's father mocks the idea that Alpine scenery should be considered conducive to study. But for Brahms, the summer of 1886, which he spent at a Swiss villa on the edge of Lake Thun, was a period of remarkable productivity. In the space of a few short months, he composed six vocal works, two violin sonatas, a piano trio and his F Major Cello Sonata.

Brahms's Second Cello Sonata is perhaps the most rhapsodic piece he ever wrote. Written for the cellist Robert Hausmann, known for his rich, powerful sound, the cello bursts forth with unrestrained ardour over the piano's tempestuous *tremolandi*.

'Passion' is the watchword of this exceptionally bold first movement: the instruments engaging in a fiery tussle. The slow movement, *adagio affettuoso* (slow and tenderly) expresses a more gentle love, before an argumentative Scherzo. The final Rondo sees a reconciliation between the soloists, despite the occasional tiff. This is 'chamber music' that smashes through the confines of the 19th-century drawing room.

Recommended recording: Jacqueline du Pré, Daniel Barenboim, Warner Classics, 1968

72

Symphony No. 3 in C Minor (1886)

Camille Saint-Saëns

Saint-Saëns was the 'greatest organist in the world' according to Franz Liszt, no slouch in the loft himself. Having taken first prize for organists at the Paris Conservatoire, he became organist at the Église Saint-Merri, before moving to La Madeleine, the premier church in Paris, in 1858. It was here, on the recently installed Cavaillé-Coll organ, with its 48 stops, four keyboards and pedals, that the musician, still in his early twenties, amazed congregations with the virtuosity of his improvisations. 'His genius was of indescribable splendour', recalled the musician Jean Huré, who heard the composer in later life:

> Following a marvellously ordered plan he improvised counterpoint in two, three or four voices with such purity and logic in the progression of parts that the most erudite musician with the most experienced ear believed that he was hearing a carefully written down composition. So difficult were certain of his impromptus that it would have taken them a year of assiduous work for our most skilled organists to play them.

Saint-Saëns's Third Symphony is, famously, 'avec orgue'. Yet while it is known as the 'Organ Symphony', the great wind instrument only makes an appearance in two of the work's four sub-sections, the same as the piano.

The first movement is reminiscent of the opening of Schubert's 'Unfinished' Symphony: nervous strings and agitated woodwind. Believing the four-movement symphonic form had the capacity to appear clumsy and disjointed, Saint-Saëns has the Allegro Moderato melting into the Poco Adagio. Here, at the start of what is really the slow movement, the organ enters, providing harmonic grounding for the lush strings. The second movement (really the third) returns to the febrile atmosphere of the first – runs on the piano adding a sense of the fantastic. Only in the final section does Saint-Saëns's unleash the true might of the organ, 'like Napoleon hurling in the Imperial Guard at Waterloo', as the playwright Lucien Augé de Lassus put it. This finale, with its memorable melody, bold brass and two pianos, is extremely well known but, despite its appropriation by Hollywood, remains indestructible. One of the most thrilling conclusions to a symphony, it is largely responsible for the fulfilment of Gabriel Fauré's prophecy that the piece would outlast the combined age of the two composers.

Recommended recording: Chicago Symphony Orchestra, Gaston Litaize, Daniel Barenboim, Deutsche Grammophon, 1976

73

The Sleeping Beauty (1888–1889)

Pyotr Ilyich Tchaikovsky

I was six years old when I was fortunate enough to be taken to a dress rehearsal of *The Sleeping Beauty* at Covent Garden. Although recovering from a fever, I was transfixed and, in the months that followed, played my cassette of the music to destruction. Several decades later and my love of Tchaikovsky in general and this ballet in particular is undimmed.

Tchaikovsky was the first composer to produce a ballet score of genius. Although the music of Adam (*Giselle*) is good and that of Delibes (*Coppélia and Sylvia*) very good, it was Tchaikovsky who raised the bar and in *Swan Lake, The Sleeping Beauty* and *The Nutcracker* created music that may stand alongside the greatest Romantic symphonies. Not that his contemporaries always appreciated his efforts. When *Swan Lake* was premiered in Moscow on 4 March 1877, the critics complained that it was 'too Wagnerian' (a favourite insult of the ignorant and unimaginative), and for several decades, whole chunks of Tchaikovsky's music were regularly substituted with the work of minor composers. It is perhaps not surprising, therefore, that a decade elapsed before Tchaikovsky agreed to undertake a second balletic commission. The subject: Charles Perrault's *La Belle au bois dormant*. 'I want to tell you at once that it is impossible to describe how charmed and captivated I am [by it],' the composer wrote to the Director of the Imperial Theatres, Ivan Vsevolozhsky. 'It suits me perfectly and I could not want anything better than to write music for it.' After receiving detailed instructions from the ballet master, Marius Petipa, Tchaikovsky began work in October 1888, completing the score in August of the following year.

Even more than *Swan Lake* or *The Nutcracker, Sleeping Beauty* is Tchaikovsky's balletic masterpiece: the most unified, stupendously melodic ballet he, or indeed anyone else, ever composed. Running through it are two antagonistic themes: the jagged, discordant theme of Carabosse – the bad fairy, determined to exact revenge for not being invited to Princess Aurora's christening – and the dream-like, lyrical theme of the Lilac Fairy, who mitigates Carabosse's curse and leads Prince Florimund to the sleeping Princess. In addition to some exquisite character pieces (Vsevolozhsky plundered Perrault's other tales to create a fantasia of fairy tale figures in the third act), there are lavish waltzes and, in the Act I 'Rose Adagio', a slow movement as powerful as any Tchaikovsky penned. Shortly after the premiere at the Mariinsky Theatre on 15 January 1890, the composer confessed to his publisher Pyotr Jurgenson, '*The Sleeping Beauty* may be the best of all my compositions.' I could not agree more.

Recommended recording: Orchestra of the Royal Opera House, Covent Garden, Mark Ermler, Sony Classical, 1990

74

Symphony No. 8 in C Minor (1884–1890)

Anton Bruckner

What could possibly surpass Bruckner's Seventh Symphony? Well, arguably, his Eighth. The last symphony Bruckner would complete, it contains all the mysticism of the Seventh, albeit in a darker hue, while also conveying a sense of the monumental, if not the apocalyptic.

Bruckner's Seventh Symphony had been the first unambiguous triumph of his life and it must have been with some degree of confidence that he sent his new work to Hermann Levi, the man who had conducted its predecessor with such success at Munich. Unfortunately, Levi could not make head or tail of the piece and rejected the score. Bruckner was devastated. Never enjoying a robust mental constitution (he spent a spell in a sanatorium in 1867), he suffered a complete psychological collapse and even contemplated killing himself. When he did recover, he not only revised his Eighth Symphony but undertook changes to several earlier works.

Most musicologists agree that the revisions, despite the

personal crisis which provoked them, improved the Eighth Symphony. After a timorous and unsettling beginning – succeeded by juxtapositions of terror and resolution – the first movement originally ended with a brass coda in a major key. In the revised version, Bruckner leaves us with desolation: the movement's death throes tapped out on the timpani. A spirited Scherzo revives the piece, before we arrive at one of the most sublime slow movements in symphonic history. Although it is the only movement for which Bruckner provides no written clue as to its meaning, the theme appears to be love and the longing for love – a sensitive subject for the composer who, despite longing for romantic companionship, never married. The finale, Bruckner wrote, was 'the most significant movement of my life'. A cathedral of sound, with all the trumpets and drums such as might attend the Day of Judgement, it offers its shattered listeners, at long last, a vision of hope; a chance of salvation.

Recommended recording: Pierre Boulez, Vienna Philharmonic, Deutsche Grammophon, 1996

75

Souvenir de Florence (1887–1892)

Pytor Ilyich Tchiakovsky

Any notion that Tchaikovsky was incapable of producing the same beautiful melodies, the same rich textures, in his chamber music as in his larger-scale works evaporates when confronted with his Sextet, *Souvenir de Florence*. Not that it was easy. Writing to his brother on 27 June 1890, the composer reported that he was working on a string sextet but was struggling, 'not for want of new ideas but because of the novelty of the form. One requires six independent yet homogeneous voices. This is unimaginably difficult'.

Despite the challenges, the sextet was finished, in draft, by the end of the month and Tchaikovsky professed himself 'terribly pleased with myself'. His doubts, however, returned once he had completed the full score. 'I shall not print it until you and your companions have learned it and corrected everything that is awkward, bad or unmusical,' he wrote to the founder of the St Petersburg Chamber Music Society, Eugen Albrecht. 'It seems to me that as music it is adequate in itself. At least, I tried terribly hard.' In the end, Tchaikovsky made several changes to the piece after hearing it, privately, in his St Petersburg apartment.

Although called a *Souvenir de Florence*, this is no picture postcard. The first movement, which begins with storm and stress, has a northern, perhaps German Romantic, feel. The third-movement Scherzo is decidedly Slavic, while the finale is reminiscent of a Russian folk dance. Where then the city of Dante and Michelangelo? The name derives, solely, from the second movement and the tune which Tchaikovsky composed during his sojourn in the city in early 1890. The rough winds of the first movement subside and we feel the warmth of Tuscany, as violin and cello intertwine in a ravishing duet that might easily belong to the opera house. The brief interlude, before the theme returns, should be played extremely quietly, Tchaikovsky stipulated, so as to be just discernible, 'like summer lightning'.

Recommended recording: Borodin Quartet with Genrikh Talalyan and Mstislav Rostropovich, Chandos, 1964

76

Cavalleria Rusticana (1889)

Pietro Mascagni

Pietro Mascagni was 26 when he heard of a competition, run
by the music publisher Sonzogno, for the best one-act opera.
The son of a baker from Livorno, Mascagni began composing
as an adolescent but had dropped out of the Milan Conserv-
atory and was currently eking out an existence as a conductor
and music teacher in Puglia. On hearing of the contest – the
deadline for which was only two months away – he threw
himself into composition. His subject was the 1884 play by
Giovanni Verga, *Cavalleria Rusticana*: a melodrama of love,
betrayal and revenge, set on Easter day in contemporary Sicily.
Years later, Mascagni would dismiss the idea that his masterpiece was simply 'jotted down, like a flicker of lightning…
gushing forth in me like a gift from Heaven'. Alas, the composer recalled, '*Cavalleria* cost me much labour.'

It was worth it. Mascagni won the competition, defeating
72 rivals, and on 17 May 1890, the opera received its first
performance at the Teatro Costanzi in Rome. The event was
a sensation. The audience lapped up the hummable, sensual

score and Mascagni took 40 curtain calls. *Cavalleria Rusticana* was performed throughout Italy and, within a year, had been presented to packed houses in Berlin, Vienna, Stockholm, London and New York. Today it is best remembered for its famous Intermezzo, yet listen to the whole opera and you realise that this is but one pearl amid a gorgeous string.

Recommended recording: Renata Scotto, Plácido Domingo, Pablo Elvira, Isola Jones, Jean Kraft, Anne Simon, Ambrosian Opera Chorus, National Philharmonic Orchestra, James Levine, RCA Red Seal, 1978

77

Symphony No. 6 in B Minor 'Pathétique' (1893)

Pyotr Ilyich Tchaikovsky

'I want terribly to write a somewhat grandiose symphony, which would crown my artistic career,' wrote Tchaikovsky to Grand Duke Konstantin Konstantinovich, one year after completing his Fifth Symphony. 'For some time I have carried in my head an outline plan for such a symphony…I hope that I shall not die without carrying out this intention.'

His first attempt was not a success. Having begun sketching ideas in May 1891, he abandoned the work in December after coming to the conclusion that there was nothing 'interesting or appealing in it'. Just over a year later, he wrote to his nephew, Vladimir 'Bob' Davydov, to say that he had had a new idea for a symphony, this time with a programme. What this programme was he would not divulge but it is possible to see the plan of what would become the Sixth Symphony in the notes he wrote for his discarded work:

The underlying essence…is *Life*. First part – all impulsive passion, confidence, thirst for activity. Must be short (the finale *death* – result of collapse). Second part love: third disappointments; fourth ends dying away...

While conceiving the ideas for the symphony, during his return journey from Paris, Tchaikovsky confessed to becoming so emotional that he frequently broke down in tears. The piece was to be unlike anything he had previously composed: a symphony 'suffused with subjectivity'. Back in Russia, he worked in a white heat of creative intensity. The first movement was sketched in just four days and, by 24 March 1893, a mere six weeks later, the entire symphony was ready in draft.

This time, Tchaikovsky was well satisfied with his efforts. 'I absolutely consider it to be the best and, in particular, the most sincere of all my creations,' he wrote to Bob. 'I love it as I have never loved any of my musical offspring.'

The first movement opens ominously: a low bassoon growling over sombre strings. The sense of foreboding is instant and does not dissipate when the violas introduce the nervous first theme. The second theme is lyrical and yearning: a melody of deep, romantic love. Then, a thunder clap! The storm breaks with the ferocity of an invading army, as the first theme reappears in the form of a violent fugue. The second movement is a waltz in 5/4 time: its lilting simplicity a stark contrast to the battle that has just ended. But the martial spirit reappears in the third movement, which, after a mustering of orchestral forces in a skittish Scherzo, embarks on a bombastic march that ends in a coda of such frantic jubilation that concert-goers frequently assume that the piece has finished and break into applause. But Tchaikovsky has not finished. The slow movement has been saved till last and is among the most tragic utterances in music: a grief-stricken Adagio that ends in anguished despair.

There has been much debate about the meaning of the Sixth Symphony, whose programme Tchaikovsky kept secret but whose title, *Pateticheskaya*, translates as 'passionate' or 'emotional'. For many, the fateful first movement and tragic finale appear to presage the composer's death which, with eerie timing, occurred just nine days after the premiere. Yet while most modern Tchaikovsky scholars dismiss this notion – much less that it represents, as some have suggested, a musical suicide note – there does appear to be something highly autobiographical about this most 'subjective' of symphonies.

Recommended recording: Berlin Philharmonic, Herbert von Karajan, Deutsche Grammophon, 1977

78

La Bohème (1893–1895)

Giacomo Puccini

The traditional subjects for opera were classical myths and ancient history. Mozart and Rossini brought more domestic (if frequently ridiculous) scenarios to the stage but by the mid-19th century grandeur was back, with Verdi plundering major works of European literature and Wagner delving deep into the grottos of Norse mythology.

Reacting against this trend and seeking to differentiate themselves from the mid-century Titans, came the movement known as *verismo*: an attempt, first in Italian literature and subsequently opera, to create a more realistic portrait of the world, including, for the first time, an interest in the lower echelons of society. The first verismo opera is traditionally cited as *Cavalleria Rusticana* – Mascagni taking his story from Verga's decidedly earthy tale of feuding Sicilian peasants. Umberto Giordano's *Mala Vita* ('Wretched life') and Ruggero Leoncavallo's *Pagliacci* ('Clowns') quickly followed (both in 1892) and soon a fashion was established.

La Bohème – Giacomo Puccini's fourth opera – is not quintessential verismo. Set in 1830s Paris, it is a self-consciously sentimental depiction of bohemian life. And yet the freezing garret, the celebration of rare luxuries such as wine and cigars, the duping of the landlord and the raucous portrayal of Parisian café life all feel wonderfully real. Debussy believed that no one had 'described the Paris of that time as well as Puccini', and *La Bohème* is surely the first opera in which a request for 'the bill' appears in music.

Fleet of foot and with wonderful characterisation and atmosphere, *La Bohème* contains some of the greatest arias of the post-Verdi era.

Recommended recording: Mirella Freni, Luciano Pavarotti, Rolando Panerai, Elizabeth Harwood, Gianni Maffeo, Nicolai Ghiaurov, Schöneberger Sängerknaben, Chor der Deutschen Oper Berlin, Berlin Philharmonic, Herbert von Karajan, Decca, 1972

79

Symphony No. 2 in C Minor (1895)

Gustav Mahler

In October 1907, Gustav Mahler was visiting Helsinki, as part
of a concert tour, when he met fellow composer Jean Sibelius.
The two men went on several walks together and it was on
one of these strolls, according to Sibelius's early biographer,
Karl Ekman, that they discussed the nature of the symphony.
The Finnish composer said that he 'admired its severity and
style and the profound logic that created an inner connection
between all the motifs'. His companion fundamentally dis-
agreed. 'No,' the Austrian composer riposted, 'the symphony
must be like the world. It must embrace everything.' Whether
apocryphal or not, this statement accurately captures Mahler's
view of what the composer Carl Czerny called 'the grandest
species of musical creation': a theory he would vindicate in ten
gargantuan works.

Mahler was the ultimate late Romantic. Believing that the
purpose of 'great art' was to penetrate the mysteries of life, he
was perpetually exploring the riddle of human existence:

Whence have we come? Wither are we bound? Is it true, as Schopenhauer says, that I willed this life before I was conceived? Why do I fancy I am free, when my character constricts me like a prison? To what purpose is all this toil and suffering? How can cruelty and evil be the work of a loving God? Will death at last reveal the meaning of life?

Suffused with death, darkness, irony, fate and struggle, Mahler's symphonies – which also incorporate the terrestrial and trivial: bird song, bugle calls, cowbells, military marches and folk music – have not always been understood or appreciated. 'One of us must be crazy and it isn't me,' declared a befuddled Eduard Hanslick after coming face to face with the composer's First Symphony. Yet to those who are mesmerised by his music – and I know few who have taken the time to listen to it who are not – Mahler's symphonies come closer to comprehending and transcending the essence of the human condition than any orchestral works since Beethoven.

In his Second 'Resurrection' Symphony, Mahler explores mortality, faith and the life everlasting. Beginning with a shuddering string *tremolo*, the monumental first movement is death: the funeral, so Mahler tells us in his programme notes of the hero of his First Symphony. As the death throes of the cellos and bases give way to the declamations of the brass, a pathos-ridden second theme, flashes of jubilation and then return, Mahler poses the questions: 'Why did you live? Why did you suffer? Is it all nothing but a huge, frightful joke?'

The second movement is a Ländler – the traditional Austrian dance which Captain von Trapp dances with Maria in *The Sound of Music*. Wistful and Schubertian, it represents a sunlit memory of the deceased, before the question of life as some cruel joke reappears in the third movement: a bitter, ironic Scherzo, climaxing with a 'cry of despair'. Only in the fourth movement, with its pleading contralto solo – 'I am from God and will return to God' – do we perceive a gleam of hope: a flame that is almost immediately extinguished by the repetition of the 'cry of despair' at the start of the finale. This is the Last Judgement. The moment when 'the earth quakes, the graves burst open [and] the dead arise'. Kings and beggars, righteous and godless march side by side in a terrifying procession towards their fate – the majesty of heaven proclaimed by trumpets and tubular bells. Finally, after one last 'cry of despair', we hear the Last Trumpet (played by an off-stage brass ensemble), before the chorus of saints enters in hushed tones: 'Rise again, yea, thou shalt rise again.' The glorious conclusion – the celebration of God's love and eternal life – is summarised in the composer's own words:

> And behold, it is no judgement; there are no sinners, no just. None is great, none small. There is no punishment and no reward. An overwhelming love illuminates our being. We know and *are*.

Recommended recording: Anna Larsson, Eteri Gvazava, Ofeón Donostiarra, Lucerne Festival Orchestra, Claudio Abbado, Deutsche Grammophon, 2003

80

Symphony No. 3 in D Minor (1896)

Gustav Mahler

For most of his adult life, Mahler's onerous conducting sched-
ule meant that the only time he had for composition was during his summer holidays. Then he would take himself off to
his tiny hut in the mountains near Salzburg and immerse himself in his music. Furnished with just a piano, desk, armchair
and sofa, he would work all morning, typically starting at six
o'clock and then go for long walks in the afternoon. These
were an opportunity for him to arrange his thoughts and be
inspired by the magnificent scenery.

Mahler had evoked the spirit of the natural world in his
First Symphony but it was in his Third that he set himself the
staggering task of capturing the whole of nature in a single
work. 'Just imagine a work of such magnitude that it actually mirrors the whole world,' he wrote to the soprano Anna
von Mildenburg. 'My symphony will be something the like of
which the world has never yet heard!'

Later, when his pupil Bruno Walter visited him at his
Alpine retreat, the composer jokingly reprimanded the young

conductor for admiring the view: 'You needn't stand staring at that – I've already composed it all!'

Even by Mahler's standards, the Third Symphony is a colossus. At 90–105 minutes (depending on the conductor), it is the longest symphony in the classical repertoire and requires some 60 string players, four flutes, four oboes, five clarinets, four bassoons, eight horns, an off-stage post horn, four trumpets, four trombones, a tuba, seven timpani, two glockenspiel, a bass drum, several off-stage snare drums, cymbals, tambourine, tam-tam, rute, six bells, a mezzo-soprano, a women's choir and a boy's choir. This is not a piece that can be produced on the cheap!

The Third is not always easy nor is it, emphatically, 'background music'. From the opening horn fanfare we are aware that this is art which is going to take us by the scruff of the neck. And yet it seems that all of life – its triumphs and its tragedies, its humour and vigour, its joy and banality – are crammed into these six, wildly varied movements. The sixth movement is especially moving. Originally entitled 'What God tells me', before being changed to 'What love tells me', and marked *langsam – ruhevoll – empfunden* (slowly, tranquil, deeply felt), it has a strong claim to be the most profoundly beautiful slow movement ever written.

Recommended recording: Leonard Bernstein, Christa Ludwig, New York Philharmonic Orchestra, Deutsche Grammophon, 1986

81

Enigma Variations (1898–1899)

Edward Elgar

'The Germans, who make doctrines out of everything, deal with music learnedly; the Italians, being voluptuous, seek in it lively though fleeting sensations; the French, more vain than perceptive, manage to speak of it wittily; and the English pay for it without meddling.' Although it is painful to admit, the French 19th-century novelist Marie-Henri Beyle, better known as Stendhal, had a point. In the two centuries since the death of Henry Purcell, in 1695, Britain failed to produce a single composer who could rival the giants of the continent (Handel became a British subject but was born in Brandenburg-Prussia). Then, at long last, came Edward Elgar.

It was after a long day's music teaching, on 21 October 1898, when Elgar lit a cigar and began to play about on the piano. After a while, his wife, Alice, exclaimed, 'Edward, that's a good tune…play it again.' So he did. Then he started to improvise: creating variations on the theme in the manner of some of the couple's friends and asking his wife to guess who was being evoked.

So were born the Variations on an Original Theme – 14 musical portraits, including the composer's wife, his friends, a friend's bull dog and, finally, Elgar himself. The most famous variation, Nimrod, depicts Elgar's close friend August Jaeger (the Old Testament king, Nimrod, was a 'mighty hunter' and *Jäger* means 'hunter' in German). Its stirring melody is often deployed as an expression of British patriotism – it is played each year on Remembrance Day at the Cenotaph – yet its inspiration was friendship and personal courage. When, a month earlier, Elgar was depressed and thought of abandoning his musical calling, it was Jaeger who rallied his spirits. Beethoven had been beset by troubles, his friend told him, and yet he continued to compose great music, 'And that is what you must do.'

But what of the enigma? Well, the enigma is the theme; the original tune which, Elgar later explained, expresses the 'loneliness of the artist'. Yet he also alluded to a deeper mystery: a theme that went 'through and over the larger set…but is not played'. For over a hundred years, musicians and musicologists have attempted to solve this riddle. Most believe that it refers to the derivation of the theme or a hidden melody, but answers have ranged from the slow movement of Mozart's Prague Symphony to 'Rule Britannia' and 'Auld Lang Syne'.

What we do know is that the *Enigma Variations*, premiered on 19 June 1899, made Elgar's name and re-established a tradition of British music that would thrive for the next 50 years.

Recommended recording: Hallé Orchestra, Mark Elder,
Hallé, 2002

82

L'histoire de Manon (1872–1919 & 1973)

Jules Massenet, arranged and orchestrated by
Leighton Lucas and Hilda Gaunt

Given that the French composer Jules Massenet wrote an entire opera based on the novel *L'histoire du chevalier des Grieux et de Manon Lescaut* by the Abbé Prévost, it may seem quixotic to include the ballet on the same subject, not specifically created by the composer but made up of a compilation of his music, arranged by the British composer Leighton Lucas and the Royal Ballet's chief accompanist Hilda Gaunt. Yet, while I like the opera *Manon*, I love the ballet.

It was the final night of the Royal Ballet's 1973 season and Antoinette Sibley was preparing to go on stage as Aurora in *The Sleeping Beauty*, when she found a book in her dressing room containing both Prévost's novel and Mérimée's *Carmen* – a buy-one-get-one-free of femme fatales. On top of it was a note from the Royal Ballet's Artistic Director and principal choreographer, Kenneth MacMillan: 'Some holiday reading for you – which will come in handy for March 7, '74.' Waiting in the wings for her entrance, Sibley asked Anthony Dowell – who had received the same book and was dancing Prince Florimund – to find out which novel MacMillan was planning to turn into a ballet. By the interval, Dowell had the answer: it was *Manon*.

Like John Cranko's *Onegin* – which uses Tchaikovsky's music but not one bar of *Eugene Onegin* – Massenet's opera is entirely absent from the score created by Lucas and Gaunt, who, instead, chose to create an elaborate miscellany of the composer's other melodies. The anti-heroine's seductive and sad theme, therefore, comes from Massenet's song 'Crépuscule' ('Twilight'), while her first *pas de deux* with the ill-fated Des Grieux is to the haunting strains of 'Élégie'. Other works that yielded tunes include the operas *Chérubin*, *Le Cid*, *Cléopâtre*, *Grisélidis* and *Don Quichotte*; Massenet's *Scènes dramatiques* and *Scènes pittoresques*; the oratorios *Ève* and *La Vierge*; and the song 'Ouvre tes yeux bleus'. If this sounds like a hotch-potch, it was the great achievement of Lucas and Gaunt to create a score of such fluidity, unity and purpose that one can easily believe that this is the ballet Massenet always intended to compose.

An anti-heroine who makes Emma Bovary look like Fräulein Maria, the character of Manon – a courtesan who entraps the impoverished aristocrat Des Grieux with her sexual allure, only to leave him for a richer man – caused a scandal when she first appeared in print in 1733. Over 200 years later, it is amusing to see how this French siren still had the capacity to enrage the critics. What 'an appalling waste of the lovely Antoinette Sibley, who is reduced to a nasty little diamond digger', complained the *Morning Star*, after MacMillan unveiled his creation on 7 March 1974. 'Basically, Manon is a slut and Des Grieux is a fool and they move in the most unsavoury company,' opined the *Guardian*. Yet while there is an element of truth behind these assertions, MacMillan's accomplishment is to make us empathise with the eponymous anti-heroine, so that by the end of the ballet we are as devastated by her premature demise as her unfortunate lover.

Recommended recording: Orchestra of the Royal Opera House, Covent Garden, Richard Bonynge, Decca, 1985

83

Tosca (1895–1900)

Giacomo Puccini

There was a time when 'serious' music lovers tended to be sniffy about Puccini. Accused of sentimentality, vulgarity, melodrama and, perhaps worst of all, popularity, he was dismissed as a composer of 'bourgeois candy floss'; the author of that 'shabby little shocker', as the American musicologist Joseph Kerman notoriously described *Tosca*. Nowadays, however, I think that most people have grown up and Puccini is widely regarded as a composer of genius; the worthy successor to Giuseppe Verdi in the Italian operatic tradition.

That *Tosca* is melodramatic is undeniable (but then so is *Rigoletto* and, in many respects, *Fidelio*). Based on the play by the French dramatist Victorien Sardou, *Tosca* is a story of love, political repression, torture and murder that conforms to the standard formulae for romantic opera: tenor loves soprano; soprano loves tenor; baritone tries to kill the former and rape the latter.

At first, Puccini felt that he was the wrong composer to bring *Tosca* to the opera house: 'I pleaded that my style was too gentle, too delicate and that my music moved on a different plane of expression,' he later explained. He need not have worried. While a lightness of touch had served him to perfection in *La Bohème*, in *Tosca* he revealed an ability to compose some of the darkest, most demonstrably dramatic music in opera. The tone is set from the opening brass chords – the *leitmotif* of the sadistic Chief of Police, Baron Scarpia – and reaches its dramatic climax in Act II, when the arch-villain offers Tosca a Faustian pact, while her lover is being tortured off-stage. A 'shocker'? Certainly. 'Shabby'? Not on your life.

Recommended recording: Leontyne Price, Plácido Domingo, Sherill Milnes, New Philharmonia Orchestra, Zubin Mehta, RCA Red Seal, 1972

84

Piano Concerto No. 2 in C Minor (1900–1901)

Sergei Rachmaninov

After the failure of his First Symphony, the 24 year-old Rachmaninov fell into a deep depression. Filled with self-doubt, his friend, Princess Alexandra Lieven, arranged a meeting with his idol, Count Tolstoy. 'You must work,' adjured the great novelist, stroking Rachmaninov's knees. 'Do you think that I am pleased with myself? Work. I work every day.' Three years later, the author of *War and Peace* was less encouraging: 'Tell me, is such music needed by anybody?', he enquired after the young man had played one of his own compostitions. Rachmaninov's creative torpor deepened. Moribund, he followed the suggestion of his cousins, the Satins, that he see a hypnotherapist. Through daily sessions with the music-loving Dr Nikolai Dahl, Rachmaninov began to regain his confidence. 'You will begin your concerto,' intoned the doctor. 'You will work with great facility. The concerto will be excellent.' Rarely can a hypnotic injunction have received so great a vindication.

Commencing with deep, swelling chords, like the tolling

of a Russian bell, Rachmaninov's Second Piano Concerto unfolds a series of melodies, each, seemingly, surpassing the last in beauty. Incredibly lush, it can seem at times that we are listening to a 1930s Hollywood score – not for nothing did David Lean choose this music for his 1945 film, *Brief Encounter* – but Rachmaninov always keeps himself within bounds, changing the mood to prevent us drowning in treacle. Not that he could stop the crooners from stealing his tunes. The second theme from the third movement provided the basis for Frank Sinatra's 'Full Moon and Empty Arms', while Eric Carmen took the theme from the second movement for his hit ballad 'All by Myself'. It remains one of the most popular and recognisable pieces of 'classical' music.

Recommended recording: Leif Ove Andsnes, Berlin Philharmonic, Antonio Pappano, EMI, 2005

85

Symphony No. 2 in D Major (1901–1902)

Jean Sibelius

From almost his first works, Jean Sibelius was extolled as the 'voice' of his native Finland. 'We recognise these [tones] as ours, even if we have never heard them as such,' wrote the critic Oskar Merikanto, following the premiere of Sibelius' symphonic poem, *Kullervo*, on 28 April 1892. For centuries part of Sweden (Sibelius's first language was, in fact, Swedish), Finland had been an autonomous Grand Duchy of the Russian Empire since Tsar Alexander's victory over the Swedes in the 'Finnish War' of 1809. Although the Finns were, indeed, afforded a measure of autonomy, Finnish nationalism grew throughout the 19th century, spurred by the publication, in 1835, of the *Kalevala* – an epic poem drawn from Karelian folklore and the basis for Sibelius's own *Kullervo*. When Tsar Nicholas II effectively abolished Finnish autonomy with the 1899 'February Manifesto', the nationalists were outraged. Some 500,000 Finns signed a petition of protest and Sibelius composed his 'Song of the Athenians' – a thinly veiled rallying cry, inspired by Athenian resistance to the Germanic Heruli tribe in 267 AD. That same year he wrote the work for which he remains best known. Although it masqueraded under a variety of different titles, in an attempt to deceive the Russian censor, there is no mistaking the patriotism at the heart of *Finlandia*.

The earliest ideas for the Second Symphony were not born of nationalist fervour. Staying in Rapallo in northern Italy during the winter of 1901, Sibelius sketched what would become the opening theme of the slow movement – a malevolent bassoon over a 'walking' *pizzicato* motif – beneath an inscription explaining that the idea derived from the thought of Don Juan opening the door of his castle to 'Death'. Later, in Florence, he wrote a second 'Resurrection' theme but by the time he returned to Finland he had decided to subsume what may have been intended as a tone poem on Don Juan or Dante's *Divine Comedy* into a new symphony.

The Second Symphony begins with the strings swaying gently, like a camera trying to realise its focus. The mood is sunny and pastoral as Sibelius embarks on a series of perfectly executed fragments that seem to evoke different aspects of the Finnish landscape – its wide expanses, dense forests and 'thousand lakes'. Occasionally a cloud comes scudding across the horizon but, broadly, the spirit of gaiety and sense of excitement remains. Talking to a pair of conductors in later life, the composer said of the beginning of the first movement: 'This theme is the most joyful I have ever written. I don't understand why it is often played too slowly.'

The atmosphere, naturally, darkens with the emergence of the 'Death' theme in the Andante – snarls of protest emerging from the brass – but a charged Scherzo provides a renewed sense of optimism, as the forces of the orchestra rush about in frantic preparation for the finale. Some Sibelius scholars have dismissed the idea, popularised by the contemporary Finnish conductor, Robert Kajanus, that the Second Symphony was directly inspired by political events in Finland. Yet, listen to the opening theme of the fourth movement, with its rich texture and heart-tugging melody, and it is hard not to conclude that this is music overflowing with love of country.

Recommended recording: London Symphony Orchestra, Colin Davis, RCA Red Seal, 1994

86

In the South (1903–1904)

Edward Elgar

Elgar's music evokes the spirit of England and the English landscape like no other. Yet it is to Italian scenery that we are indebted for the composer's stirring tone poem, *In the South* – the subtitle, 'Alassio', refers to the town on the Italian Riviera where, with the help of 'Tomaso Cooko', the Elgars were holidaying during the winter of 1903–1904.

He was an inveterate walker and it was on one of the composer's daily perambulations that inspiration struck. 'We had climbed one of the *salitas* (the steep paths that scar the hills) and came suddenly upon a little chapel by a group of pine trees', recorded the Elgars' travelling companion Rosa Burley.

> Classical in style, like a temple, it was falling into ruin and the sudden impact of its beauty silenced us.
>
> 'It really only needs a shepherd with his pipe to make the picture complete,' I said.
>
> At that moment, to our amazement, a shepherd did in fact appear from behind the chapel. He was dressed in a sheepskin

and unconcernedly drove his flock along the path and out of sight.

'In a flash,' recalled the composer, who had already been dreaming of Caesar's legions crossing the extant Roman bridge over the river, 'it all came to me – the conflict of the armies on that very spot long ago, where I now stood – the contrast of the ruin and the shepherd – and then, all of a sudden, I came back to reality. In that time I had composed the overture – the rest was merely writing it down.'

Despite this provenance, *In the South* – which sweeps along on great gusts of passion – seems, to my ear, more redolent of the Malvern Hills than the Mediterranean. Perhaps Elgar was homesick (he had recently been forced to give up the tenancy of his beloved Worcestershire cottage)? Perhaps it was the rain and gales that reminded him of his native land? Or perhaps it was simply a case of being able to take the man out of England but not England out of the man? Whatever the explanation, it does not detract from a musical panorama with few parallels.

Recommended recording: Hallé Orchestra, Mark Elder, 2002

87

The Merry Widow (1905)

Franz Lehár

Not everything has to be deep. Sometimes it is fun to skim the cream off the coffee; to admire the gilt on the gingerbread; to lose oneself in a world of balls, champagne and social comedy. Operetta emerged in Paris during the 1850s as a reaction to the dominance of grand opera and the increasingly serious projects of the Opéra Comique. Light and melodic, with spoken dialogue, dances and popular songs, its undisputed early master was Jacques Offenbach, before Johann Strauss II and Franz von Suppé gave the genre a Viennese twist in the 1870s.

Franz Lehár spent the first decade of his career serving the Habsburg monarchy as a bandmaster for various infantry regiments, as well as the naval corps stationed at Pola. A composer of waltzes and marches, he left the army in 1902 and took up the position of conductor at Vienna's Theater an der Wien, the stage that had hosted the premieres of both *The Magic Flute* and *Fidelio*. Here, he presented his operettas *Wiener Frauen* and *Der Rastelbinder* (1902) – both of which were successful – as well as *Der Göttergatte* and *Die Juxheirat* (1904) – a brace of failures.

Lehár was not the first choice to compose the music for *Die Lustige Witwe* ('The Merry Widow'), the operetta created by Victor Léon and Leo Stein from the play *L'Attaché d'Ambassade* by Henri Meilhac (one-half of the writing team that produced *Carmen*). Originally given to Richard Heuberger – a composer who, ironically, had prevented Lehár from gaining the post of conductor of the Vienna Municipal Orchestra, on the spurious grounds that he did not know anything about waltzes – it passed to the former bandmaster when Heuberger failed to come up with the goods. 'Please give me *The Merry Widow*; I simply must do it!' the 35-year-old composer pleaded, before playing Léon the Act II duet 'Dummer, dummer Reitermann' ('Silly, silly cavalier') down the telephone. He got the commission and the public got the most successful operetta in history, with 422 performances in German-language theatres in its first 18 months, rising to a staggering 18,000 by January 1909.

A love story that revolves around the attempts of Count Danillo, the attaché at the Pontevedro Embassy in Paris, to secure the fortune of a rich widow for his country (a thinly disguised Montenegro), *The Merry Widow* is filled with boisterous dances, lusty choruses and melodious arias. Although undeniably 'light', there are moments of real beauty, and the attraction of the music is evidenced by the range of leading musicians who have contributed to recordings, including Elisabeth Schwarzkopf, Joan Sutherland, Nicolai Gedda, Cheryl Studer, Bryn Terfel, Herbert von Karajan and John Eliot Gardiner. Even Mahler loved Lehár's creation. Returning from the theatre, he and his wife danced to its tunes and played its waltzes from memory on the piano. Unable to remember one passage, they visited Vienna's principal music shop but felt embarrassed to be seen purchasing so 'popular' a score. Thus, while Mahler distracted the shopkeeper with questions about his own publications, Alma surreptitiously browsed the score of *The Merry Widow*. By the time they left the shop, she was able to sing the entire waltz to her husband in the street.

Recommended recording: Cheryl Studer, Boje Skovhus, Barbara Bonney, Rainer Trost, Bryn Terfel, The Monteverdi Choir, Vienna Philharmonic, John Eliot Gardiner, Deutsche Grammophon, 1994

88

Symphony No. 2 in E Minor (1906–1907)

Sergei Rachmaninov

It was not that Rachmaninov's First Symphony was simply a flop; it received the sort of critical mauling that would cause most people to give up show business:

> If there is a Conservatory in Hell and one of its gifted pupils should be given the problem of writing a programmatic symphony on the Seven Plagues of Egypt and if he should write a symphony resembling Mr Rachmaninov's symphony – his problem would have been carried out brilliantly.

Thus declared the vituperative César Cui. Worse, the piece failed to satisfy its author. 'I am not at all affected by its lack of success, nor am I disturbed by the newspapers' abuse,' wrote Rachmaninov, a trifle disingenuously, to the composer Aleksandr Zatayevich, 'but I am deeply distressed and heavily depressed by the fact that my Symphony, though I loved it very much and love it now, did not please me at all after its first rehearsal.'

Notwithstanding the success of his Second Piano Concerto it was, therefore, with more than a degree of apprehension that the composer began work on a new symphony, in Dresden, during the autumn of 1906.

To begin with, Rachmaninov was dissatisfied with his efforts. 'No more symphonies. Curse them!' he expostulated to fellow composer Nikita Morozov. 'I don't know how to write them, but mainly I don't want to. My second work is slightly better than the [First] Symphony but still dubious in quality.' Not for the first time, the composer was being egregiously self-critical. Rachmaninov's Second Symphony constitutes the zenith of late Russian Romanticism. After a languorous introduction – one long orchestral sigh – the composer begins to flesh out the opening 'Motto' theme. Despite the dominance of the strings, the sound is rich and full. Despondent then yearning, meditative then stormy, Rachmaninov carries us on deep orchestral waves towards the tempestuous Scherzo. With a sense of urgency, if not outright panic injected, we are then permitted to luxuriate in what is, without doubt, the composer's most lyrical slow movement, a theme of overflowing love that borders but does not descend into schmaltz. The finale is delightfully boisterous: a bravura performance that wholly belies the composer's lack of confidence in his symphonic abilities.

Premiered on 2 February 1908, the Second Symphony received widespread acclaim and won Rachmaninov a second Glinka Award. Commenting on the piece, the critic Yuli Engel argued that it proved the 34-year-old composer a 'worthy successor to Tchaikovsky':

After listening with unflagging attention to its four movements, one notes with surprise that the hands of the watch have moved 65 minutes forward. This may be slightly overlong for the general audience, but how fresh, how beautiful it is!

Recommended recording: Royal Concertgebouw Orchestra, Vladimir Ashkenazy, Decca, 1983

89

Symphony No. 9 in D Major (1908–1909)

Gustav Mahler

In his Ninth Symphony, Mahler confronts death in all its sorrow and mystery. A recurring theme in his too brief life, it came to the fore in the summer of 1907, when a combination of scarlet fever and diphtheria robbed him of his elder daughter. Both parents were, naturally, distraught and a physician was called to care for Mahler's wife, Alma. Having attended to the grieving mother, the doctor examined the composer. A faulty heart was diagnosed. 'The verdict,' Alma later wrote, 'marked the beginning of the end for Mahler.'

The long-standing debate about the relationship between an artist's life and his/her works gains piquancy with Mahler's Ninth. The traditional interpretation, overwhelmingly influenced by Alma's less than reliable memoirs, is that the composer, following his diagnosis, became fixated on his impending demise and reflected this in his music. The Ninth Symphony, it has been variously suggested, is a premonition of the composer's death; a funeral for the symphony; a farewell, even, to tonality. Against these interpretations stands the fact that Mahler went on to work on another symphony after completing the Ninth, as well as letters, which indicate that the composer was far from finished with either life or music.

Perhaps the most important thing to remember, therefore, is that music, more than any of the arts, is manifold. A single phrase may contain a variety of meanings; an entire symphony – particularly one by Mahler – comprises a universe of thoughts. That Mahler Nine brims with pathos is obvious from the opening bars: the halting rhythm in the basses and harp, reminiscent of a tolling bell or, perhaps, a faltering heart. The first-movement Andante has a pastoral feel, but whether it is the meadows descending from the composer's hut in the Tyrol or the Elysian Fields that are being evoked is open to question. While much of the movement resembles a resigned farewell, there are also stirring climaxes, which sound like a pleading for life.

The next two movements are dances: the angry Rondo-burlesque dedicated to the critics who had sniped at Mahler's music for years. But it is in the final movement that we encounter the work's emotional core. A heart-broken Adagio, which quotes from Beethoven's 'Les Adieux' Sonata, Mahler pours out his love for life while, simultaneously, displaying a serene courage in the face of death. The long, long *diminuendo* at the end of the work is marked *ersterbend* ('dying away') and, beneath that, the composer has written, 'Farewell! Farewell! /O Beauty! /Love!' Mahler died on 18 May 1911. He never heard his Ninth Symphony performed.

Recommended recording: Berlin Philharmonic, Claudio Abbado, Deutsche Grammophon, 1999

90

Violin Concerto in B Minor (1909–1910)

Edward Elgar

Thanks, in large part, to Jacqueline du Pré, Elgar's Violin Concerto has been somewhat overshadowed by his Cello Concerto. For my money, however, the Violin Concerto concedes nothing to its more famous sibling in depth, lyricism or originality.

It was the celebrated Austrian violinist Fritz Kreisler who urged Elgar to write the Violin Concerto. Speaking to the *Hereford Times*, in October 1905, he advertised his admiration for the English musician:

> If you want to know whom I consider to be the greatest living composer, I say without hesitation Elgar...I place him on an equal footing with my idols, Beethoven and Brahms...His invention, his orchestration, his harmony, his grandeur, it is wonderful. And it is all pure, unaffected music. I wish Elgar would write something for the violin.

Immediately, Elgar began to sketch ideas but it was not until the summer of 1910 that the concerto was finished. Although the violin had been Elgar's instrument in his youth, he consulted his friend W. H. Reed, the future leader of the London Symphony Orchestra, on bowing and other technical points, while also incorporating some minor suggestions of Kreisler's. 'I will shake Queen's Hall!' declared the violinist and, by all accounts, he did. The enthusiasm was 'unbounded', recorded the composer's wife, after the premiere on 10 November 1910. Kreisler, despite one slight mistake, excelled himself and Elgar conducted the LSO with assurance and sensitivity.

The Violin Concerto belongs to a different world from Elgar's earlier compositions. Written in the first decade of the 20th century, when many of the certainties of the Victorian era were starting to fray, the piece has an ambiguity, which prevents us from labelling it 'happy' or 'sad'. What cannot be denied is the intensity of the emotion. (Elgar thought it might be 'too emotional'!) Amazingly rich in texture and thematic variation, the overwhelming sense is one of love: its grandeur, tribulations, triumphs and yearnings. On the manuscript, Elgar has left the tantalising inscription: *'Aqui está encerrada el alma de...'* ('Herein is enshrined the soul of...') We do not know the identity of the soul that is enshrined in the work but the most likely answer seems to be Alice Stuart-Wortley, a friend for whom the composer had developed an unconsummated passion. When Elgar, finally, conceived the theme linking the primary and secondary subjects in the first movement he christened it 'Windflower' – a flora that could withstand the winds of self-doubt and the pet-name he, thereafter, used for Alice.

One of the most challenging pieces in the repertory, it may

also be the most romantic violin concerto ever written.

Recommended recording: Renaud Capuçon, Simon Rattle, London Symphony Orchestra, Erato, 2020

91

The Firebird (1910)

Igor Stravinsky

Igor Stravinsky was the *enfant terrible* of early-20th-century 'classical' music. Scandalously discordant and violent, his primeval ballet *The Rite of Spring* caused a near riot when it was premiered at the Théâtre des Champs-Élysées on 29 May 1913. Objects were thrown at the orchestra, scuffles broke out and around 40 concert-goers were ejected from the hall. Although it appears that the tumult was sparked as much by Vaslav Nijinsky's brutalist choreography as Stravinsky's score (the orchestra was soon drowned out in any case), there is no escaping the shocking, revolutionary nature of the music. 'I was convinced he was raving mad,' recalled the conductor Pierre Monteux after hearing Stravinsky's initial rendition of the ballet on the piano. The *London Musical Times* was no less baffled: 'To say that much of it is hideous as sound is a mild description…Practically it has no relation to music at all as most of us understand the word.' (I confess that I am with the *Times* critic on this one!)

The Rite of Spring was Stravinsky's third collaboration with the Russian impresario Sergei Diaghilev. After the runaway success of his first season of Russian ballet in Paris (1909), Diaghilev was eager for new works that he could present the following year. The idea of a Russian folk ballet, based on a fusion of the Firebird myth and the fairy tale *Koschei the Deathless*, had been gestating within his circle for some time and, shortly after the 1909 season, the hunt was on for a composer. Having tried several more established (and conventional) composers, Diaghilev turned to the young man whose orchestral fantasy *Fireworks* he had heard and admired.

The Firebird shows the influence of Stravinsky's teacher, the recently deceased Nikolai Rimsky-Korsakov. Coruscating and insistent, with the richest of orchestrations, Stravinsky's score succeeds wonderfully in painting the story of the Prince who, with the help of the Firebird, rescues a gaggle of princesses from the clutches of an evil sorcerer. Although Richard Strauss believed the young Russian had made a mistake by beginning his ballet quietly, it is hard to imagine anything more ghoulish than the introduction, with the cellos and basses stalking up and down an octatonic scale. Trills and string *glissandos* (slides) signal the first flash of the Firebird, as it flits about the stage, trying to evade its pursuer. After a traditional *pas de deux*, Stravinsky points the way to the future with a pulsating 'Infernal Dance' – still one of the most exciting ensemble pieces in ballet. The work ends in a blaze of light: the freshly liberated princesses celebrating the triumph of good over evil to the frenzied sounds of the brass and triangle.

Recommended recording: Antal Dorati, London Symphony Orchestra, Mercury, 1959

92

Der Rosenkavalier (1909–1910)

Richard Strauss

Where to go with opera after Wagner? The creator of *Tristan und Isolde* and *The Ring* was a mountain over which no composer could climb. 'But,' Richard Strauss laughingly explained to his collaborator, the novelist Stefan Zweig, 'I have helped myself by making a detour round him.' And by God, he did! In *Salome* (1905) and *Elektra* (1909), Strauss scandalised audiences with his cacophonous depictions of two larger-than-life femme fatales, before turning, in *Der Rosenkavalier* (1911), *Ariadne auf Naxos* (1912/1916) *and Arabella* (1933), to romance and social comedy.

Der Rosenkavalier is Strauss's tribute to Mozart and the Vienna of Maria Theresa. Set to a libretto by the poet and playwright Hugo von Hofmannsthal – with whom Strauss had already worked on *Elektra* and, in one of the great creative partnerships, would go on to collaborate on *Ariadne auf Naxos, Die Frau ohne Schatten* and *Arabella* – it is a madcap comedy with moments of great poignancy. The music is sumptuous and deliberately anachronistic. Although set in the mid-18th century, the sparkling waltzes and fertile melodies reflect the Vienna of Strauss's youth, vindicating the composer's observation that 'sentimentality and parody are my line of country'.

The trio at the end of Act III is one of the most sublime ensembles in the operatic repertory (the only direct rival would be the trio from Act I of Mozart's *Così fan tutte*). According to family legend, the composer was playing the piece on the piano, searching for a resolution, when his wife, the great soprano Pauline de Ahna, cried out, 'Go on, go on!' 'Isn't it getting too long?' Strauss asked. 'No! Go on, go on!' Thirty-nine years later, the trio was performed at the composer's funeral, under the baton of the 36-year-old George Solti. Three of Germany's leading sopranos took part but, as the soaring, overlapping lines arched over the orchestra, each was overwhelmed and broke down in tears.

Recommended recording: Elisabeth Schwarzkopf, Christa Ludwig, Teresa Stich-Randall, Otto Edelmann, Eberhard Wächter, Philharmonia Orchestra, Herbert von Karajan, Warner Classics, 1956

93

An Alpine Symphony (1900–1915)

Richard Strauss

From Vivaldi to Beethoven, Wagner to Messiaen, myriad composers have been inspired by the natural world. None, however, in my opinion, succeeds in evoking the mysterious majesty of nature as well as Richard Strauss in his *Alpine Symphony*.

It was while Strauss was waiting for a new libretto from Hugo von Hofmannsthal, in the spring of 1911, that he confessed to 'torturing myself with a symphony – a job, when all is said and done, that amuses me even less than chasing maybugs'. Indeed, he had been torturing himself for some time. The earliest sketches for what would become *An Alpine Symphony* were made around the turn of the century; a musical response, the composer's notes tell us, to the suicide of the artist Karl Stauffer-Bern. Although Strauss abandoned the work, which he originally planned to call *Der Antichrist: Eine Alpinesinfonie* – a direct reference to Nietzsche's 1888 work – he took it up again upon hearing of the death of Mahler in May 1911. 'The death of this aspiring, idealistic, energetic artist [is] a grave loss,' he wrote in his diary. A loather of metaphysics, Strauss felt it was an indictment of his age that the Jewish Mahler had been obliged to convert to Catholicism in order to secure his post as Musical Director of the Vienna Court Opera. 'It is clear to me that the German nation will achieve new creative energy only by liberating itself from Christianity,' he wrote. 'I shall call my alpine symphony *Der Antichrist*, since it represents moral purification through one's own strength, liberation through work, worship of eternal, magnificent nature.' Although some of these philosophical aspects were watered down (including the title) over the next four years, it is possible to view the finished work as an allegory of the artist's struggle against society and with his own creative genius.

An Alpine Symphony is not, in fact, a symphony but the last of Strauss's tone poems. Lasting some 50 minutes, it consists of 22 seamless parts, each depicting a different phase of a journey through the Alps. The music is amazingly evocative: you can actually hear the snow glinting in the moonlight in the opening night section, while the portentous intonations from the brass sketch the great mountain looming before us. After a glorious sunrise – every bit as powerful as Strauss's more famous evocation in *Also Sprach Zarathustra* – we begin our ascent with a lively march in the strings, the off-stage French horns representing a distant hunt. We delve deep into a forest, wander by a brook and pause by a waterfall, as the harps and woodwind cascade in glittering droplets.

On the Alpine pasture, we listen to the birds calling, while the tinkle of cowbells may be a direct echo of Mahler's Sixth Symphony. Having taken the wrong path and struggled through some thickets and undergrowth, our arrival on a glacier is signalled by the entry of the organ. It gets distinctly hairy as we begin our final assault – the *pizzicato* and shrieks from the clarinets suggestive of unstable footing – but we make it to the summit and are rewarded with a recapitulation of the 'Sun' theme, now in golden C major. This is the emotional heart of the piece: the achievement of man and the glory of nature.

But it is not over. We have to get down and, during the descent, are caught in a storm. Strauss's storm blast is truly terrifying: the sunny themes from earlier in the piece distorted with dissonance, as the raging elements chase us down the mountain. The penultimate section entitled '*Ausklang*' ('final' or 'closing chorus') has a hymn-like quality; the composer inviting us to reflect on our exertions. It is loving, tender music, which Strauss asks to be played 'in gentle ecstasy'. The poem ends where we began: the 'Night' theme drawing a veil over the world, while the brass proclaims, one last time, the indomitable mountain, just visible against the inky sky.

Recommended recording: Andris Nelsons, City of Birmingham Symphony Orchestra, Orfeo, 2010

94

Symphony No. 7 in C Major (1924)

Jean Sibelius

Unlike many great composers, Sibelius had a remarkably long life. Born in the mid-19th century, he died on 20 September 1957, at the age of 91. During the last 30 years of his life, however, he hardly composed a note. Retreating to Ainola, his house near the village of Järvenpää, he began what became known as the 'Silence of Järvenpää': a self-imposed creative abstinence, during which he did not even like to talk about music.

The Seventh Symphony was among the last pieces Sibelius composed before retreating from the world. Written between 1923 and 1924, it was conceived at a difficult time for the composer. He was grieving for his recently deceased brother, while pouring vast quantities of whisky down his throat in an effort to calm his nerves and stay his shaking hands.

One afternoon in the spring of 1923, before he was due to conduct a concert of his own music in Gothenburg, he went missing. After an extensive manhunt, he was found, at eight o'clock, swilling champagne and knocking back oysters in a restaurant. Dragged to the concert hall, he made it onto the podium but after a few bars stopped the orchestra, apparently under the illusion that it was a rehearsal. Sibelius's wife, Aino, was mortified. She never attended another of his concerts and, after watching him struggle to write his Seventh Symphony, bottle in front of him, she wrote him a pleading letter:

> You must change or it will be the end of you. Try to get rid of whatever it is that pulls you down there. Have you not seen where it is taking you? Even if you complete a work or two, they are nothing compared to what you could achieve.

Although he failed to heed this advice, Sibelius's Seventh Symphony is widely regarded as the most significant achievement of his life. Originally entitled *Fantasia sinfonica*, it consists of one extraordinary movement of changing colours, shifting moods and contrasting textures. It begins with what should be the most innocent, indeed, anodyne, start to any piece of music: a rising C major scale. A rising C major scale that, with the timpani roll and *crescendo*, feels threatening and which is capped by a dissonance, not unlike the famous chord from the opening of *Tristan und Isolde*. From this point, we realise that we are in a strange sound world where grief mingles with nostalgia, innocence is shaded by melancholy and anxiety vies with peace.

In the years following the premiere of the Seventh, Sibelius tried to compose an eighth symphony but, ultimately, abandoned the attempt. We can only speculate as to the reason why but there are more ridiculous explanations than to suggest that the composer realised he had said all he wished to say.

Recommended recording: Osmo Vänskä, Minnesota Orchestra, BIS, 2015

95

Concerto in F (1925)

George Gershwin

George Gershwin introduced classical music to the Jazz Age. Born in New York in 1898, the son of Russian-Jewish emigrés, he started playing the piano at the age of ten and by 15 was earning $15 a week working as a 'song plugger' (someone employed by music publishers to promote their music by continually playing it) – in Manhattan's Tin Pan Alley. Within a year he had published his first song and, in 1918, was signed by music publishing firm T. B. Harms as a song composer. It was an astute hire. Gershwin's song, 'Swanee', recorded by Al Jolson in 1920, enjoyed a nine-week run at the top of the US charts and sold over two million records and one million copies in sheet music.

The success of 'Swanee' established Gershwin as one of the leading lights of Broadway. He had, however, been classically trained and, as he later confessed, always wanted to 'work at big compositions'. His chance came when the legendary bandleader Paul Whiteman persuaded him to write a quasi-concerto for piano and jazz band. Composed in just five weeks, 'Rhapsody in Blue' brought jazz rhythms to the concert hall and Gershwin to the attention of serious music critics. It also led to a commission. On 13 February 1924, the day after the premiere of 'Rhapsody in Blue', no less a figure than the Director of the New York Symphony Orchestra, Walter Damrosch, contacted Gershwin with a request for a full-blown piano concerto.

Even more than 'Rhapsody in Blue', the Concerto in F represents the perfect fusion of jazz and classical. Scored by Gershwin for full symphony orchestra ('Rhapsody in Blue' had been orchestrated by Whiteman's arranger, Ferde Grofé), it exhibits all the vitality and syncopation of jazz, while retaining the structure and form of the classical concerto.

The piece kicks off with great thwacks on the timpani, while the horns introduce the Charleston rhythm that will recur throughout the first movement. Alternately quick and pulsating, romantic and sentimental, this movement, Gershwin wrote, symbolises the 'young enthusiastic spirit of American life'.

The second movement is a sultry blues number, a solo trumpet setting the 'poetic, nocturnal atmosphere'. But there is little time to slumber. The third-movement Rondo starts violently and comprises an 'orgy of rhythms' deployed at break-neck speed.

Reflecting on the concerto after its creator's death in 1937, Arnold Schoenberg – famed as the pioneer of atonality – commented that Gershwin was both 'an artist and a composer':

What he has done with rhythm, harmony and melody is not mere style…The impression is of an improvisation with all the merits and shortcomings appertaining to this kind of production...He only feels he has something to say and he says it.

Recommended recording: Stefano Bollani, Riccardo Chailly, Leipzig Gewandhaus, Decca, 2010

96

Viola Concerto in D Minor (1928–1929)

William Walton

When Sir William Walton appeared on *Desert Island Discs*, just after his 80th birthday in 1982, he was delightfully self-deprecating. Discussing his years as a choirboy at Christ Church, Oxford, the presenter, Roy Plomley, asked how he had managed to remain at Oxford after he had completed prep school. 'Well, they didn't know what to do with me,' claimed Walton. What actually happened was that Thomas Strong, the kindly and musical Dean, had become aware of the boy's talent. One Sunday, after morning Eucharist, the young Walton had presented Strong with a bundle of his compositions. 'It so happened,' recalled Strong, 'that the examinations for music degrees were going on just then and [the eminent composer Sir Hubert] Parry was staying with me. He picked up Walton's manuscripts and was interested. I remember his saying, "There's a lot in this chap, you must keep an eye on him!"' Strong, who was already paying the balance of the boy's school fees, did as he was told. He wrote to Walton's father and, having obtained his assent, enrolled Walton as an undergraduate at Oxford's most distinguished college, despite his being just 15 years old.

The idea for the Viola Concerto came from the conductor Thomas Beecham, who, in 1928, suggested that Walton write something for the celebrated violist, Lionel Tertis. Although Walton claimed to know little of the instrument, he agreed and was soon enthused. 'I finished yesterday the second movement of my Viola Concerto,' he wrote to his friend, the poet and memoirist Siegfried Sassoon, on 2 February 1929. 'At the moment it is my best work, better than the *Sinfonia* [Concertante], if only the third and last movement works out well...' Unfortunately, Tertis did not agree and refused the opportunity to premiere the piece. Years later, he admitted what a colossal blunder this had been:

> With shame and contrition I admit that when the composer offered me the first performance I declined it. I was unwell at the time; but what is also true is that I had not learnt to appreciate Walton's style. The innovations in his musical language which now seem so logical and so truly in the main-stream of music then struck me as far-fetched. It took me quite a time to realise what a tower of strength in the literature of the viola is this concerto...

After a brief period of doubt, during which he contemplated transforming the work into a violin concerto, Walton regained his confidence when the German composer and violist Paul Hindemith agreed to perform the piece. The premiere, at one of Sir Henry Wood's promenade concerts, on 3 October 1929, vindicated him spectacularly. 'Walton was 'a young composer of quite exceptional gifts', proclaimed the *Sunday Times*, while *The Times* praised the works innovation, 'subtlety', 'rhythmic vitality' and 'lyrical charm'. (One explanation for the latter quality is found in the dedication 'To Christabel' – this being Christabel McLaren, later Lady Aberconway, with whom Walton was in love at the time).

Not everyone liked it, however. Despite his clear influence on the piece, Elgar could not stomach the concerto. Listening to Walton conduct the work with the penitent Tertis at the 1932 Three Choirs Festival in Worcester, the older composer was heard to deplore the fact that 'such music should be thought fit for a stringed instrument'. Later, Walton, who worshipped Elgar's music but had never met its author, found himself standing next to the great man in the gents' lavatory. 'I want to say how much I admire your work and your conducting,' he stammered. Elgar smiled politely. 'Most kind! And do you happen to know what [horse] won the three-thirty at Worcester?'

Recommended recording: James Ehnes, BBC Symphony Orchestra, Edward Gardner, Chandos, 2017

97

Symphony No. 5 in D Minor (1937)

Dmitri Shostakovich

How can art survive when freedom perishes? How, indeed, do artists survive? These fundamental questions dominated the career not only of Dmitri Shostakovich but of every genuine composer, novelist, poet and painter forced to live under the hammer of Stalinism.

It was on 16 January 1936 that the Soviet dictator, accompanied by a pod of apparatchiks, attended a performance of Shostakovich's opera, *Lady Macbeth of Mtsensk*. Not only had the work been a popular success, it had won the approval of the cultural commissars. Shostakovich's opera, it was claimed, was 'the result of the general success of Socialist construction'. But Stalin did not like it. Twelve days after the performance, an article appeared in the official Soviet newspaper, *Pravda*, denouncing the opera for its 'deliberate dissonance', 'musical chaos' and cacophony of 'quacks, grunts and growls'. Shostakovich was accused of serving up 'Leftish confusion instead of natural human music' and, even more damagingly, a 'petty-bourgeois "formalist" attempt to create originality'. The composer's fall was instantaneous. Critics who had lauded *Lady Macbeth* retracted their praise, commissions dried up and the premiere of his Fourth Symphony was cancelled. Wretched and fearful, Shostakovich lay low before seeking musical atonement for his 'sins'.

Shostakovich's Fifth Symphony rehabilitated him. More conservative than the Fourth (which would not receive its orchestral premiere until after Stalin's death), it was accepted as 'a Soviet artist's practical creative reply to just criticism'. Yet while the Fifth Symphony appears to be a genuine attempt to appease the regime, it may, in fact, have been subversive. In the year since Shostakovich's denunciation, Stalin had initiated the 'Great Purge', resulting in the deaths of millions of so-called 'enemies of the people'. The third, slow movement of the Fifth Symphony is a grief-soaked lament of such sublime pathos that people wept openly at the premiere. Years later, when Shostakovich was asked about the symphony, he is alleged to have replied: 'Of course they understood, they understood what was happening around them…'

Recommended recording: Leonard Bernstein, New York Philharmonic, Sony Classical, 1959

98

The Adventures of Robin Hood (1938)

Erich Wolfgang Korngold

'If my books had been any worse,' declared Raymond Chandler, author of *The Big Sleep*, 'I should not have been invited to Hollywood, and if they had been any better I should not have come.' Erich Korngold, by contrast, would always be glad he came to Hollywood. Indeed, it saved his life.

Erich Wolfgang Korngold was a child prodigy like few others. In his earliest years, he was composing works of astonishing maturity; pieces that, even then, seemed modern. It 'had a peculiarly chromatic streak and was saturated with dissonances, departing from all norm', recalled Korngold's father, an eminent music critic, of his eight-year-old son's cantata, *Gold*. When Gustav Mahler heard the piece, he pronounced Erich 'a genius!'

Two years later, Julius Korngold sent a selection of his son's compositions to a small group of musical experts. The response was unanimous. 'This is completely phenomenal,' exclaimed the conductor, Arthur Nikisch. 'As to modernity and virility of style, the only analogy that springs to my mind is that of the young Handel,' declared Germany's foremost musicologist. The letter from Richard Strauss was particularly pleasing:

> The first feeling one has when one realises that this was written by an 11-year-old boy is that of awe and concern…This assurance of style, this mastery of form, this characteristic expressiveness…this bold harmony, are truly astonishing.

Korngold came to the public's attention through *Der Schneemann* ('The Snowman'), the ballet-pantomime he composed at the age of 11. His first, full orchestral piece, the *Schauspiel Ouvertüre*, was composed at 14; his first operas, *Der Ring des Polykrates* and *Violanta*, at 17. With *Die Tote Stadt* ('The Dead City'), written in his early twenties, he briefly overtook Strauss as the most performed German-language composer in the world. A sumptuous opera that reveals the influence of Puccini, as well as Strauss, *Die Tote Stadt* was dropped from the repertoire following the rise of National Socialism (Korngold was Jewish) but, in recent years, has enjoyed something of a revival.

In 1934, Korngold travelled to Hollywood to work on a reorchestration of Mendelssohn's music for Max Reinhardt's *A Midsummer Night's Dream*. The following year, he composed his first original film score for *Captain Blood*, starring Errol Flynn and Olivia de Havilland, and gained an Oscar nomination.

His symphonic approach to the silver screen amazed Tinseltown and, in January 1938, while waiting in Vienna for the premiere of his opera *Die Kathrin*, he received an urgent call to return to Hollywood to compose the music for *The*

Adventures of Robin Hood, also starring Flynn and de Havilland. It was a fateful summons. Two months after Korngold's departure, Hitler's troops crossed the border and Austria was subsumed into the German Reich. Had Korngold remained in Vienna and failed to escape, he would, almost certainly, have ended up in a death camp. *The Adventures of Robin Hood* saved his life.

Faced with having to supply more than 80 minutes of film music in short order, Korngold decided to base his score on *Sursum Corda*: a grand symphonic overture he had written when he was 22. Although gloriously iridescent, with a heroic trumpet theme, the piece had been one of the composer's rare flops and was even booed at its premiere. One suggested reason for its failure is the sheer abundance of musical ideas within the work. If, however, this was a problem, it was a good problem to have and one that Korngold was now able to turn spectacularly to his advantage.

Widely regarded as the high point of Hollywood symphony writing, *The Adventures of Robin Hood* is really one gigantic tone poem or, as Korngold liked to think of his film scores, 'opera without singing'. There are leitmotifs for each of the main characters, passages of extraordinary rhythmic vivaciousness to accompany the many fight scenes and a melting love theme for Maid Marian and the eponymous hero. Although Korngold's music reflects the action to perfection, close your eyes to the men in green tights revelling in what Korngold called the 'flirt-feast' scene in the middle of the film and you could be waltzing in *fin de siècle* Vienna.

Filmed in glorious Technicolor and costing an eye-watering $2 million, *The Adventures of Robin Hood* was a smash at the box office and earned Korngold his second Academy Award for best original score.

Recommended recording: William Stromberg, Moscow Symphony Orchestra, Naxos, 2003

99

Romeo and Juliet (1935–1940)

Sergei Prokofiev

Despite competition from Bellini, Berlioz, Gounod and Tchaikovsky, no piece of music, in my view, succeeds in capturing the ecstasy and agony of Shakespeare's tragic love story as well as the ballet by Sergei Prokofiev.

Composed at the Bolshoi's bucolic retreat of Polenovo, during the summer of 1935, *Romeo and Juliet* was conceived at a pivotal moment in the composer's life. Having left Russia after the 1917 Bolshevik Revolution, Prokofiev worked in the USA and Paris, where he collaborated with Sergei Diaghilev and his Ballets Russes. During the late 1920s, however, he began to undertake concerts within the Soviet Union and, by the middle of the following decade, had all but decided to relocate his family to Stalin's Russia, just when most right-minded people were trying to go the other way. Why Prokofiev wished to take this extraordinary step is not entirely clear. He may have been homesick. He may have been politically naïve. Or, he may have believed there were advantages to be gained from a regime that was prepared to make enticing offers, like a commission for a grand ballet at Moscow's Bolshoi Theatre.

If the latter was the case, it was not long before the wool was removed from the composer's eyes. Having completed the piano score of *Romeo and Juliet* by 8 September 1935, Prokofiev found that Soviet officials had their doubts about his ballet, in particular the alternative happy ending, which he had devised with his collaborators Sergei Radlov and Adrian Piotrovsky. 'Our own Shakespeare scholars proved more papal than the Pope,' the composer commented acerbically.

Then there were political events. In January and February 1936, Pravda denounced Shostakovich not only for *Lady Macbeth of Mtsensk* but also for his ballet *The Limpid Stream*. This was not the time to mount complicated new works with controversial endings and the Bolshoi management decided to cancel the planned staging of *Romeo and Juliet*. Dejected and frustrated, Prokofiev resorted to rearranging his score into two orchestral suites. Their success revived interest in the original ballet and, after a somewhat muted premiere at the Brno State Theatre in Czechoslovakia, *Romeo and Juliet* was finally presented in Leningrad on 11 January 1940.

The ballet that was performed at the Kirov Theatre (formerly the Mariinsky) was notably different to the original. Not only was the Shakespearian tragic ending restored but the choreographer, Leonid Lavrovsky, demanded additions as well as changes to the score. Fresh variations for the tragic lovers were composed, whole numbers were cut or reorchestrated and a 'Morning Dance' was added to the opening scene. This latter augmentation was especially controversia: Prokofiev refused to provide extra music for the *corps de ballet*, so Lavrovsky resorted to pilfering a Scherzo from the composer's

Second Piano Sonata. When Prokofiev dropped into rehearsal and discovered this act of piracy, he was furious. 'You have no right to do a thing like that…I am not going to orchestrate that number.' 'Then we shall have to play it on two pianos,' retorted Lavrovsky. Prokofiev gave in.

Despite the artistic bickering, the delayed Russian premiere of *Romeo and Juliet* was a triumph. The celebrated prima ballerina Galina Ulanova danced the title role and received rave reviews, as did Lavrovsky's choreography and Prokofiev's score. *Romeo and Juliet* became a showpiece of the Soviet balletic repertoire and earned Prokofiev the Stalin prize – a not insignificant decoration, since it offered some protection from the gulag. Since then, there have been over 14 rechoreographed productions, including Kenneth MacMillan's acclaimed 1965 version for the Royal Ballet.

Recommended recording: Valery Gergiev, London Symphony Orchestra, LSO Live, 2008

100

Four Last Songs (1948)

Richard Strauss

The world changed more during the course of Richard Strauss's life than during the chronology of any other composer mentioned in this book. Born in 1864, before Germany existed as a nation, he lived to see his country desecrated and dismembered prior to his death on 8 September 1949. Between these dates, he lived through and witnessed the unification of Germany under Bismarck, the militarism of Kaiser Wilhelm II, the horrors of the First World War, the febrile hedonism of the Weimar Republic, the rise of National Socialism, the destruction of the Second World War and, finally, the occupation and partition of his homeland by the victorious Allies.

Nor was the transformation in music any less radical. Raised in the age of Wagner and Brahms, Strauss died in the era of Schoenberg, Messiaen and atonality. For a while he had been seen as the apostle of modernism – 'a serpent I've harboured in my bosom', according to the Kaiser. In *Salome* and *Elektra*, his revolutionary handling of harmonics, including the free use of chromatics and dissonance, both shocked and fascinated contemporaries. But then he took a different turn and composed the Mozartian *Der Rosenkavalier*. For 'retrograding' to the wigs and chandeliers of 18th-century Vienna and the sound-world of his childhood, Strauss was frequently attacked but he never accepted the premise of the criticism:

> Modern? What does 'modern' mean? Give the word a different significance! Have ideas like Beethoven's, write contrapuntally like Bach, orchestrate like Mozart and be genuine and true children of your own times, then you will be modern!

Strauss's final years were filled with sadness and anxiety. Desperate to protect his family from the Nazis (his daughter-in-law was Jewish), he was later castigated over his links with the regime. Strauss was no Nazi and detested the persecution of the Jews, which he considered 'a disgrace to German honour'. He was, however, naïve and allowed himself to be exploited for propaganda purposes. His jejune belief that, as an artist, he could somehow levitate above politics is summed up in a letter he wrote to Stefan Zweig:

> Do you believe I am ever, in any of my actions, guided by the thought that I am 'German'? Do you suppose Mozart was consciously 'Aryan' when he composed? I recognise only two types of people: those who have talent and those who have none.

Forced to undergo a denazification trial (which cleared him of all charges), the 81-year-old composer and his wife – the once-formidable soprano, Pauline – slipped into self-imposed exile in Switzerland. There, despite being comfortable, he felt gloomy and moribund. He continued to be attacked over his association with the Third Reich and lacked a project to distract him. One day, in early 1948, his son said to him: 'Papa, stop writing letters and brooding...Write a few nice songs instead.' Six months later, when his son and daughter-in-law were visiting him, the composer walked into their room and placed some scores on the table: 'Here are the songs your husband ordered.'

Strauss' *Four Last Songs* have been the object of so many superlatives that it is virtually impossible to describe them without falling into cliché. Almost the last compositions he wrote, they are the ultimate vindication of his belief that 'Art is the finest gift of God that exalts over all earthly suffering and our beloved music is the most delightful'. A celebration of the soprano voice (the sound closest to Strauss's heart), they are also a tribute to Pauline, his wife and muse of 54 years. Particularly affecting, in this respect, is his setting of Joseph von Eichendorff's 'Im Abendrot' ('In the Sunset'), which tells of an old couple who, 'through sorrow and joy', have wandered 'hand in hand' and are now 'at rest from our wanderings /now above the quiet land'. With the exception of 'Frühling' ('Spring'), all deal with the coming of death – after the final line of 'Im Abendrot' ('Is this perhaps death?'), horn and strings quote the theme from the composer's youthful tone poem *Death and Transfiguration* – and yet there is not one note of despair. Rather, Strauss wraps the listener in the sublime beauty of his music and reflects on a life well lived. Although deeply personal – Strauss admitted that he himself was at the centre of almost all of his musical ideas – the *Songs* may be seen to have a wider musical significance as a defence of tonality; proof that music, despite the discords of the world, could still be beautiful; a demonstration that the classical tradition lives on.

Recommended recording: Jessye Norman, Leipzig Gewandhaus, Kurt Masur, Philips, 1982

Glossary

Adagio – Tempo marking (Italian for 'at ease'), meaning that the music should be played slowly

Allegro – Tempo marking (Italian for 'lively'), meaning that the music should be played in a brisk, up-beat manner

Andante – Tempo marking (Italian for 'walking'), meaning that the music should be played at a walking pace, neither too fast nor too slow

Appassionato – Italian for 'passionate', meaning that the music should be played passionately

Aria – An individual song, typically in an opera

Atonal – Music in which no key can be discerned; characterised by dissonance

Baroque – The period of music between c. 1600 and 1750, comprising composers such as Monteverdi, Purcell, Handel and Bach

Chromatic – Typically, harmonic structures which derive from the 12-note chromatic scale, which is formed entirely of semitones. If played on the piano, a chromatic scale would involve playing all of the black notes as well as the white notes in sequential order.

Classical – The period of music between c. 1750 and 1820, comprising composers such as Haydn, Mozart and Beethoven (though Beethoven also opens the door to the Romantic period)

Crescendo – A dynamic instruction: to play, gradually, more loudly

Coda – The final flourish or conclusion of a piece or section of music

Diminuendo – A dynamic instruction: to play, gradually, more quietly

Fugue – A contrapuntal composition in which a short melody or phrase is introduced before being taken up, successively, by other parts (voices, instruments, musical lines), which develop and interweave

Forte – A dynamic instruction: to play loudly

Fortissimo – A dynamic instruction: to play very loudly

Largo – Tempo marking, meaning to play very slowly

Libretto – The text of an opera or vocal work

Lied(er) – German for song(s)

Modernist – Period of music between c. 1910 and 1975, comprising composers such as Stravinsky, Schoenberg and Shostakovich

Piano – A dynamic instruction: to play quietly

Pianissimo – A dynamic instruction: to play very quietly

Pizzicato – To pluck the strings on stringed instruments, as opposed to using a bow

Presto – Italian for 'quickly', meaning that the music should be played at a fast tempo

Romantic – The period of music between c. 1820 and 1910, comprising composers such as Verdi, Wagner and Tchaikovsky

Scherzo – A lively, skittish piece of music or movement (typically a third movement) from a symphony

Tremolo – The very fast repetition of a single note to produce a 'trembling' effect

Acknowledgements

My first and greatest thanks must go to my editor, Evie Dunne of Short Books, who persuaded me to turn a lockdown project for friends into something more substantial. Evie's patience and skill as an editor are equalled only by her talents as an artist – a fact evidenced by her superb illustrations. To her colleagues at Short Books – Rebecca Nicolson, Aurea Carpenter, Helena Sutcliffe and Paul Bougourd – I am inordinately grateful: for their enthusiasm for the project and for the tireless work which took this book from commission to publication in seven short months. Although the views contained and any errors are mine and mine alone, I would like to express my sincere thanks to Jonathan Gaisman QC for reading the manuscript and bringing his considerable expertise to bear. I would like to thank my uncles, Andrew Gilmour and the conductor Oliver Gilmour, for sharing their extensive knowledge of music and the pianist and composer Harriet Petherick Bushman for answering various technical questions. My agent, Bill Hamilton, provided support with his usual calm sagacity, while Ned Dunne helped with the playlist. My parents, Jane and Peter Pleydell-Bouverie, did me the great service of proof reading my 'essays' as they emerged, skilfully fielding my dyslexia. Although they are responsible for almost all of the few things that I have got right in my life, I would like, in particular, to record my heartfelt thanks to them for playing classical music when I was a child and encouraging my enthusiasm. Finally, I would like to thank the friends who received the original essays. Their companionship cheered me during a bleak winter and I look forward to many warm summers of friendship to come.

Please find the accompanying playlist on Spotify:
Perfect Pitch – Tim Bouverie
https://spoti.fi/3kMWsRc

Or scan the QR code: